SET YOUR

FAMILY

free

OTHER DESTINY IMAGE BOOKS BY BOB LARSON

Jezebel: Defeating Your #1 Spiritual Enemy
(ISBN 978-0768407068)

Curse Breaking: Freedom From the Bondage of Generational Sin
(ISBN 978-0768403299)

Demon Proofing Prayers: Bob Larson's Guide to Winning Spiritual Warfare
(ISBN 978-0768439304)

Dealing with Demons: An Introductory Guide to
Exorcism and Discerning Evil Spirits
(ISBN 978-0768409673)

SET YOUR
FAMILY
free

Breaking
SATAN'S ASSIGNMENTS
Against *your* Household

DR. BOB & LAURA LARSON

DESTINY IMAGE® PUBLISHERS, INC.

P.O. Box 310, Shippensburg, PA 17257-0310

"Promoting Inspired Lives."

This book and all other Destiny Image and Destiny Image Fiction books are available at Christian bookstores and distributors worldwide.

For more information on foreign distributors, call 717-532-3040.

Or reach us on the Internet: www.destinyimage.com

ISBN 13: TP 978-0-7684-1224-6
ISBN 13 EBook: 978-0-7684-1225-3
HC ISBN: 978-0-7684-1538-4
LP ISBN: 978-0-7684-1539-1

Cover design by Eileen Rockwell
Interior design by Terry Clifton

For Worldwide Distribution, Printed in the U.S.A.
1 2 3 4 5 6 7 8 9 10 11 / 20 19 18 17

DEDICATION

To Bob, without whom I could never have had such a dynamic and rewarding life. You are the engine propelling our family to seek God with all our hearts, use our gifts to serve our Father, and honor the Lord in everything. You are so talented, kind, and hardworking. I am truly thankful for you, and I love you.

To our daughters Brynne, Brooke, and Brielle—you make me who I am and my love for you is endless! When you were born, I sought the mantle of intentional motherhood, asking the Lord to provide me with His divine wisdom as well as the stamina and determination to be the best mother for you beautiful young ladies. Thank you for growing and stretching me, and for encouraging me with your love and care in return.

To my own dear mother, Joan, with great love and gratitude for your devotion as a single parent and your encouragement to follow Jesus. Thank you for always loving me and for your kind words. You are my best role model for motherhood.

To the families we have been blessed to minister to, thank you for your trust in us and your hard work to save your families. It is worth all the sacrifices and struggles to behold families that are truly set free!

LAURA LARSON

To you, Laura—you make my half whole. With you and the Lord I can be strong to fight for our family. It is true that opposites attract, and yet in many ways we are so much alike—and you complement the areas where I am weak. The books I've written in the past two decades of my life were possible because of your love and encouragement. God knew that I needed a special partner who could handle all the long hours of ministry and travel, someone who could be a strong mother when I'm gone and yet bond with me closely when I'm home.

To you, my three daughters, who have stretched my faith since I first held your tiny bodies in my arms—that awesome call to fatherhood has molded my character as nothing else could. To kneel by your beds each night to bless you with prayer has been more important to me than any other accomplishments.

To my parents, who long ago went to be with the Lord, with warm recollections of our simple family life on the Nebraska farm: You weren't perfect parents, but you did love God, and that heritage has been handed down to me to carry on. I look forward to seeing you again in Heaven to rejoice in what God did with such inauspicious beginnings.

I also thank all of you who have turned to us for help and guidance. Your trust in our calling from the Lord is humbling; your determination to fight back against all the odds of hell has made every investment of time and energy worthwhile. As individuals and families, together we have sought the hope that is in Christ, made possible by his great sacrifice upon the cross.

BOB LARSON

CONTENTS

READER'S GUIDE

Bob Larson

It will be helpful to the reader to understand the approach we have taken in this book. Listed below are guidelines by which the information has been compiled and organized.

1. This is not a book about deliverance and exorcism, though many of my other books have focused on this topic. It is assumed that those readers wanting to look further into more specific aspects of spiritual warfare will consult those books. We have listed several of them below, in descending order with the latest at the top:

   - *Dealing with Demons: An Introductory Guide to Exorcism and Discerning Evil Spirits*

   - *Jezebel: Defeating Your #1 Spiritual Enemy*

   - *Curse Breaking: Freedom from the Bondage of Generational Sin*

   - *Demon-Proofing Prayers*

   - *Larson's Book of Spiritual Warfare*

   - *Larson's Book of World Religions and Alternative Spirituality*

2. When we speak of "deliverance" we refer collectively to all that is involved in the process of setting a person free from demonic bondage; thus, deliverance includes inner healing work and various prayers of curse-breaking, as well as approaches to forgiveness and reconciliation. "Exorcism" is the act of expelling an evil spirit, the final step in the deliverance process. A deliverance minister is any concerned Christian, usually a lay person, who feels called to engage in the spiritual calling of exposing and casting out demons.

3. The true identities of the individuals referred to in cited case studies have been changed. None of the real names are the same as those used in the telling of these stories.

4. On occasion the facts of more than one case have been combined, when the essence of the account is not compromised by this literary device.

5. Several theological assumptions are foundational in the approach of spiritual warfare that Laura and I embrace. First, Christians can be demonized. Secondly, all believers in Jesus have conferred authority to confront demonic forces and expel them in the name of Jesus.

6. This book is primarily intended for a Christian readership, though those of other faith positions, or no faith, will find the advice on these pages to be practical. There are many references for seeking spiritual help and counseling assistance. We believe that biblically based counseling, which is founded on scriptural principles of the Word of God, is preferable; however, they are many fine secular therapists who are skilled in marriage and family intervention. Each

couple in crisis must determine for themselves which counselor best meets their needs and seems effective in addressing the differences that divide.

7. Deliverance and exorcism are normative to Christian belief and living. Our International School of Exorcism has several courses devoted to an intense study of church history. The courses reveal how integral to early Church life the casting out of demons was. Many troubled marriages need both wise counsel and some form of deliverance prayers so that all aspects of spiritual and relational deficiencies are addressed.

8. If intervention by means of deliverance is necessary, such spiritual help is mandated by Christ. We take seriously the fact that the Great Commission of Mark 16:15–17 declares that the first sign of the Gospel's integrity and authenticity is the demonstration of Christ's command, "In my name they will cast out demons."

9. Our intended audience is husbands and wives who are seeking help to correct a problematic marriage or a family system at some level of crisis. Pastors and counselors will also find this book helpful, as it arises from decades of hands-on experience with families in bondage to both human and supernatural hindrances.

Laura and I have collaborated on the writing of this book. At times, I speak directly as the voice of a specific chapter or portion of a chapter. Laura does the same. Certain chapters have our voices intermingled. In some cases, we speak together, using the "we" pronoun. This book is a mutually creative process; its ideas and concepts have sprung from our ministry as well as our home lives as parents. We speak from experience as spiritual counselors and deliverance ministers. We also share from the perspective of a mom and dad. Our viewpoints are influenced by the fact that I have been in active ministry for four decades, and Laura has been a full-time homeschool mom to three daughters. As of the writing of this book, our oldest, Brynne, is in her final year of premed, preparing to be a doctor. Our middle child, Brooke, is in her first year at university with plans to be a lawyer. Our youngest, Brielle, is a sophomore in high school. We have been happily married for twenty-four years.

This book follows a template designed to bring families and individual family members to a place of liberation in every area of life. This underlying pattern isn't always explicit, but it guides our thought processes and the things we wish to emphasize by our writing. The implied guide that we use is as follows; bringing a family from bondage to freedom is a ten-step process:

1. Recognition that a problem exists with either the family dynamic or individual members, or both.

2. Confronting the challenges within the family system and making each member aware, if they are of a cognizant age, that what ails the home cannot continue.

3. Agreeing to seek help outside the familial structure.

4. Approaching the appropriate spiritual overseers, such as pastors, and making them aware that issue(s) exist and help is being sought.

5. Identifying suitable sources of help within the Christian community and finding assistance through professional intervention.

6. Subordinating individual agendas to the greater good of the family by a willingness to receive and act upon qualified advice.

7. Assenting to continue this process until solutions are in place that will heal the home.

8. At some point, receiving what's known as spiritual "inner healing" to supplement the therapeutic process.

9. If necessary, undergoing deliverance prayers and possibly exorcism to rid demonic barriers to wholeness of the family.

10. Continuing accountability to therapeutic and spiritual authority to be certain that resolution has been reached and the family has been truly set free.

In pursuing this course of action, there are several common impediments that we have encountered that seem to be barriers to finding help and implementing solutions. First, the initial refusal of one or more family members, usually a spouse, to cooperate. Second, the idea, at least within the Christian community, that Jesus will "take care of it" and so there is no need to expose family foibles to the outside world. Third, that just praying about it for a spiritual solution will solve things. Finally, that professional intervention via a counselor, therapist, or doctor is somehow not spiritual and therefore an offense to God.

Let's carefully analyze the faulty "magical thinking" that pervades these stubborn obstructions:

Someone won't cooperate. This is a huge hurdle, especially if the objection is from the top-down. Parents can usually insist on the cooperation of minor children. But if the husband/father is not on board, there may need to be immediate intervention from an authority figure, such as a pastor, to insist that action be taken. We have had cases where a wife has been forced to seek legal advice and even begin separation procedures before her husband will agree to seek help. If the wife won't cooperate, the husband must be steadfast, but loving, in his stand as the spiritual head of the home.

Don't worry, Jesus will solve it. This is the "magical thinking" that we refer to. Yes, Christians understand that Christ is the ultimate answer to all things in life. But the Lord uses many things to guide His children on the path to freedom. Included in His plan may be medical doctors, psychiatrists, social workers, clergy, licensed counselors (which we'll address later in this section), and wise extended family members or mature Christian friends.

Prayer fixes everything. We could write page upon page listing Bible verses that point out the importance of acting upon our prayers. The Book of James, for example, lays out the importance of deeds to back up faith, especially when caring for those in need: "Faith, by itself, if it does not have works, is dead" (James 2:17). In dealing with a case of incest in the Corinthian church, Paul tells the believers to take action regarding this moral blight, not just to pray about it. "Deliver such a one to Satan for the destruction of the flesh," Paul admonishes.[1] Prayer is important, but we must put hands and feet to our prayers.

Help from a professional counselor isn't spiritual. Here's the underlying issue with this objection: The person who is objecting may really be afraid that the solution will be too specific, too clinical. Mental illness might be detected. Hidden agendas could be exposed. Specific actions might be required. One of the names applied to Christ in the messianic passage of Isaiah 9:6 is "Counselor." Christ is a counselor. A successful professional, whether he knows it or not, will emulate the Lord in the use of this title. Here are three principles that the counselor will follow:

1. He or she will seek to identify with the pain that the family is going through. Hebrews 4:15 tells us that Christ was in "all points tempted as we are." Jesus has empathy for our problems, as does any good counselor.

2. A good counselor will also comfort. Second Corinthians 1:4 tells us that the Lord "comforts us in all our tribulation, that we may be able to comfort those who are in any trouble."

3. Luke 4:18 tells us that Christ has come to *"heal the brokenhearted."* That is also what a good counselor does. Counseling is in the word of God. Christ is our ultimate counselor, of course. But just as the Lord saves us through those who share the Gospel with us, He also heals through those who have been wisely trained in the best techniques to help families faced with predicaments.

More about Isaiah 9:6. Verses six through seven of Isaiah chapter nine are quoted every Christmas, but the import of these words should remain with us all year long. The messianic titles given to Christ provide a path to families that need to be set free. We've already pointed out the importance of His title as Counselor. But He is also called "Everlasting Father." Every family needs a father, both an earthly father and a heavenly father; in this case, Jesus Christ is an eternal Father, from everlasting to everlasting. As the Son, He is one with the Father. He is the Father of life as we know it now and of the everlasting world to come. As our Father-God, the Lord expresses the qualities that an earthly father must seek to emulate: goodness, knowledge, strength, dependability, worthiness; He is the originator of peace and harmony in the home. If husbands and fathers would heed this calling, as exemplified by the person of Christ revealed in Isaiah 9:6, Christian homes would be well on their way to freedom.

INTRODUCTION

Laura Larson

Most parents would throw themselves in front of a speeding locomotive, face down a charging bear, or rip apart a pack of dogs to protect the lives of their children. They would bristle at the thought of allowing any harm to come to them, especially at their own hands. Most parents, unless they are mentally unstable, would never cause needless trauma, toxicity, or grief for their little loved ones. Parents dream of the day they will have a family, and when that family arrives they pray earnestly for their children. They seek the Lord's wisdom in their parenting. They want nothing less than the very best for their children.

But all too many Christian parents haven't reckoned with one simple fact of spiritual warfare: The enemy of our souls roams around like a roaring lion "seeking whom he may devour" (1 Peter 5:8). Satan wreaks havoc if left unchallenged. To apply the biblical metaphor—just as a physical boundary is needed to ward off an actual lion, we need appropriate spiritual boundaries to protect our children from the devil. Even when parents proactively use biblical knowledge to raise spiritually equipped children, that doesn't mean the war for the hearts and minds of their offspring will automatically be won. The sincerity of a parent's intentions won't necessarily produce strong, overcoming faith in the lives of their children.

Today, the number of people who describe the family home of their childhood as having provided love, security, and happiness is part of a rapidly shrinking minority. A tragically large number of adults look back on rough beginnings, even prior to puberty. Many have the physical and emotional scars to prove it. They were robbed of their destinies. Instead of being raised with the expectation of a future for which they were emotionally and spiritually prepared, they find themselves in midlife requiring counseling and spiritual ministry to heal many years of emotional pain and suffering. They spend large sums of hard-earned money on therapists to achieve any sense of happiness and joy. Certainly, childhood is idealized in movies and advertisements, but for many the reality is painful memories, haunting regrets, and inescapable guilt that in some way they must be at fault for their life's failures.

This book tackles several perplexing dilemmas: Why is there such disparity between what good parents want and the way that their best intentions go awry? Why do so many people from "good homes" describe their childhood as being miserable, with the happy times greatly overshadowed by bad events?

Parents who would grapple with a mountain lion to save their kids thoughtlessly turn on their own flesh and blood to shred their self-esteem. Stress, pent-up frustration, and a generationally inherited predisposition to verbal abuse make them utter regrettable statements such as, "I wish I'd never had you," or "You are a disgusting loser just like your Grandpa," or "You just aren't worth my time." Sometimes the invectives are far worse. A single statement such as this can overwhelm a child with deep feelings of inadequacy. A belated, regretful, "I'm sorry," cannot always heal the child's pain and broken trust. Even more difficult to overcome is the injury inflicted by emotional neglect, physical mistreatment, and sexual abuse.

These people are trying so hard to be good parents, with so few parenting skills passed on to them by their own parents. And while there is no such thing as perfect parenting, understanding spiritual warfare and applying its principles can give moms and dads a much better chance to create the home and family that they seek.

One of the first tasks in acquiring a spiritual warfare perspective is to be realistic and take a hard look at previous generations and inherited family predispositions. Resolving the negative spiritual influences of one's ancestors removes a huge hindrance to success, making parents stronger in the Lord and less likely to pass along even more generational damage. Breaking the bondage of old, negative behaviors and getting personal healing themselves helps emotionally and spiritually handicapped parents to do the job they otherwise couldn't do.

My husband, Bob Larson, has ministered one-on-one to thousands of people. These individuals often share gut-wrenching stories of their childhoods. They have realized that they must seek peace and freedom from their painful beginnings along with the sabotaging self-talk and all-out evil attacks. I have been honored to have helped in hundreds of such ministry sessions. Hearing people's personal stories of indescribable pain has touched me beyond words at times. I still pray for many of them today. Often, during such ministry sessions, my tears flow along with theirs as I imagine them as young children, desperate to be loved, to be affirmed, and to feel secure.

Many of these people could be described as having come from good homes, if one looked only on the outside. Despite seeming successful, they were suffering silently because of the stigma the Christian community places on someone who is in immense emotional pain. Too many Christian teachers and preachers tell us that we are to be super-spiritual, happy, thin, stylish, rich, successful, always having it altogether all the time. It is somehow the fault of the less-than-perfect believer if everything isn't seamless. Just claim you are going to be happy and you will be happy, right? Isn't that how it works? Isn't that what spirituality is all about?

The lies that some Christians believe are summed up in the suggestion that if you are not happy, something is wrong with you. Don't you have enough faith? The devil throws in even more self-condemnation. This mentality encourages people to gloss over their pain and to pray that it will go away because that's the "spiritual" thing to do. Then the Enemy inserts the biggest lie, "It's all your fault anyway."

Instead of being steeped in condemnation, those who have had a damaged childhood should be encouraged to revisit their pain and allow Christ to heal it. When people allow Jesus access to their deepest hurts, to recognize the truth about where they came from, and to break all the legal rights Satan has assigned to that distress, true, sustained freedom can come. Emotional pain is very complicated and often there are many layers. Unfortunately, even the first layers of suffering may never be faced because confessing spiritual torment is taboo in our Christian world today. This avoidance allows Satan even more opportunities to inflict the body of Christ with spiritual disfigurement.

Not everyone stays bound. I admire the broken people who pour their hearts out to my husband every day. They lay themselves completely open to his ministry, and by God's grace he helps them, investing countless hours and applying his wealth of experience. I am in awe of the courage of these people who are willing to confront their deepest torments, and I am in awe of Bob's wisdom, insight, and anointing. The Enemy, knowing their potential, may have targeted these people with an intricate plan of destruction, but God has other plans.

The enemy comes to kill, steal, and destroy (see John 10:10), and he often goes after the Kingdom's finest. Many people come from "good" homes where their parents started out with the best intentions, but somehow they allowed the devil to enter. As a result, these well-intentioned parents undermined their own children. Yet, there is hope. Those who sincerely seek the Lord eventually attain freedom, healing, and deliverance.

We call these times of intense spiritual intervention Personal Encounter sessions. Although we know that God has a sovereign plan for every individual life, I find it difficult to understand why good people, especially innocent children, must suffer so much. Then Bob reminds me that people perish "for lack of knowledge" (Hosea 4:6). This truth applies especially to parents. Knowledge of spiritual warfare is often what they lack most. Bob and I are writing this book because we felt compelled to share what we have learned through many years of ministry.

It helps to understand how most wounded people arrive at such a place of immense distress. Most of the time, the source of pain is from the family of origin. When parents don't confess their mistakes and make them right, their children often repeat the same mistakes. Failing parents, when confronted with their poor actions, must be helped to make changes and to learn to parent intentionally with freedom from generational curses.

This book explains how mothers and fathers can learn to effectively parent by using the principles of spiritual warfare to protect their children from demonic attacks. Here are some of the lessons you will take away as you discover ways to set your family free:

Understanding how generational evil plagues successive generations. You will learn how to break every curse from your children's lives and give them a clean spiritual slate. There is more than one reason to research your family tree. We have found many instances in our own family histories where the enemy could have had an open door to attack our present lives. In response, we broke all curses, both from the past and any potential curses. You can do this too. Break the curses, and it is a done deal. Shut the door to the devil. How simple and how freeing is that? For example, a family might say it is just a coincidence that their firstborn children always die early in every generation. Perhaps it's coincidence. Or it could indicate that early death is a curse. Is it worth the risk to wait and see if that will happen in your children's generation?

Parenting with a purpose in mind. We'll give suggestions to identify a purpose and plan for your child's life. Parents need to plan how they are going to raise their children before they are born. You need unity between both parents in advance, so that you will not make decisions on the fly. For example, an important decision is whether or not to homeschool. We have done it with our three children, and we'll give guidance about it later in the book. You must also decide what kind of spiritual training you'll give to your children, and how they will be disciplined. Parents need to encourage their children's gifts and to acknowledge that God has a plan for each of their lives. We are not just passing time here on earth; each of us has a unique destiny to fulfill. How will you help your child find his or her purpose in life? Will you show them how to seek God's will so that they will clearly understand on their own how to hear from Him?

The importance of a spiritual warfare perspective. Parents can help thwart the enemy's plan for their children by giving them a solid foundation in spiritual warfare, equipping them with the tools to survive in our ever-dangerous world. They need to understand the confusion in today's culture between what is good and pleasing in God's sight and what is spiritually hazardous.

If parents are hazy about what is of God and what is truly of the devil, how is a child going to have a firm foundation for strategic spiritual warfare? If a child is allowed to compromise early, it is tough to get them back on track. Spiritual warfare skills are as necessary as the three Rs of education. Children must be shown by a godly example that you take evil seriously. Live in opposition to pagan culture. Establish godly standards with boundaries in entertainment and "screen time."

Speaking blessings over your children. We'll teach you how to speak blessing over your children's lives with words that edify. It is so much easier to tell them how they have failed, but parents need to learn how to communicate blessings to their children instead. Learn how to give your children the gift of God's assurance and purpose of salvation and faith even before they are old enough to understand it. Early on, tell them who they are in the Lord and all about God's promises. Develop in them a winning attitude toward themselves and their future. Let them know that they are not losers in the Lord, but victors through Jesus.

Praying spiritual warfare prayers over children, even before they comprehend the significance, is a key to successful parenting. (Bob details this in his book *Demon-Proofing Prayers.*)

Practicing positive parenting. Stay current on parenting strategies. Know how to deal with the high-tech world and get expert advice. Abandon outdated, stereotypical Christian parenting, which can be described as strict, legalistic, and stifling. Protecting and equipping is completely different from being protective, but leaving them exposed and vulnerable. Children need to have the tools to navigate in the world, and yet not be part of it.

Being a godly example to your children. Every Christian parent needs to be a great example to their children, demonstrating consistency with Christian beliefs. There is nothing more corrosive to your parental authority than to say one thing and then do another. The apple doesn't fall far from the tree and you don't want yours tinged with hypocrisy. There is no substitute for being actively involved in your children's lives. If both parents are forced to work, make sure that the children are accountable to an approved authority figure. Children must be prohibited from forming soul ties with bad people. Sow good quality time with the Lord by leading studies that everyone participates in. Pray together and give God the glory for what he is doing in your lives.

Properly preparing your children for life. Equip your children with knowledge regarding what they believe and why. Guide them in developing healthy boundaries. If you decide, for any reason, not to homeschool your children as we recommend, please consider a Christian school as an alternative. If they go to public school, make sure they are strengthened by a solid Christian youth group and that you keep tabs on their peers. We talk in this book about intentionally parenting your children. If you had an unhappy childhood and experienced toxic parenting, actively work to change the effect of your personal history by putting forth the effort to make things different for your children. Enlist a mentor to hold you accountable. Seek professional spiritual counsel and possibly inner healing and deliverance. Research and study to devise a plan for how you would like to raise your children. It may not feel comfortable at first, but with hard work and diligence you will be able to pass along a different parenting pattern to your children.

How abusive issues affect parenting skills. When a child is abused the effects are severe. In his article, "Adverse Childhood Experiences Affect Adult Behaviors," Keir McDonald cites evidence from studies that point out the following:

> Adverse childhood experiences negatively affect adult life, says a recent study by the Centers for Disease Control (CDC). One in four young adults [was] severely maltreated during childhood and approximately half of adults in England have suffered an adverse experience during their childhood.[2]

The results of childhood abuse and neglect are recognized the world over by the psychiatric community. The effects range from addiction problems to suicide. It is a plague that our nation faces due in part to growing economic stress, family deterioration, and media distractions. Secular psychiatrists, the Centers for Disease Control, and those in the therapeutic community agree that a bad childhood typically leads to a bad adult life. And what happens when those with a terrible upbringing eventually become parents themselves?

Even more significant are the unknown spiritual ramifications of such abuse. What can harm people in this life is far overshadowed by what can compromise people's lives for eternity. The untreated spiritual ramifications of a traumatic childhood are potentially an emotional explosive that can detonate with disastrous effects. Spiritually, the effects of a traumatic childhood are deep, generational wounds that open the door to many other negative experiences and behaviors.

HOPE

This introduction might make parenting sound dismal, but there is hope. By learning to parent intentionally and purposely, you can prevent traumatic childhood experiences from reoccurring in your own children. You can learn to be a purposeful parent who understands how to right the wrongs of the past and to carry out the good spiritual journey that starts the day that each family member embraces faith in Jesus Christ as Lord and Savior.[3]

ENDNOTES

1   1 Corinthians 5:5
2   Keir McDonald, "Adverse Childhood Experiences Affect Adult Behaviors," *Psych Central* (2014). Retrieved on January 9, 2017, from http://psychcentral.com/blog/archives/2014/06/28/adverse-childhood-experiences-affect-adult-behaviors/
3   See Philippians 1:6.

Chapter One

HIGHWAY TO NOWHERE

Bruce and Jennifer Smith were a nice enough couple. Everyone in their church thought so. More than that, they seemed to be the epitome of spiritual rectitude. Jennifer headed a weekly Bible study group and Bruce met with a men's prayer breakfast every other week. They even believed fervently in deliverance, which isn't always that accepted in many church circles; nevertheless, they often prayed with other couples to be freed from spiritual bondage. They were the go-to people in their church when it came to matters of spiritual warfare.

It all looked so good, and in many ways, it was. Bruce and Jennifer did help a lot of people and lives were changed by their intervention. They gave good advice and blessed many couples with encouragement and prayer. How could anything that seemed to be so good go so bad?

CHRISTIAN COUPLE IN FOR A SURPRISE

It didn't happen overnight. They were busy for the Lord. Nothing wrong with that, at least on the surface. They were there every time the church doors were open. Who could fault such sacrificial dedication?

Neither of them was ever too busy to stop whatever they were doing to counsel someone in need. God certainly must have been pleased with their lives. Except that He wasn't. At least not when it came to certain matters of spiritual inconsistency. And it wasn't until they ended up in my office, for a Personal One-on-One Encounter, that the truth unraveled.

Ironically, they didn't come for themselves. They came for their sixteen-year-old son, James. He was exhibiting "rebellion," and they looked to me for advice to get past their little bump-in-the-road parenting crisis. "Straighten out James" was their mandate.

They weren't overbearing. After all, these were loving godly parents. They just felt that my help with some midcourse adjustments to the relationship with their son would get things back to "normal." What these parents didn't realize was that the entire family was on a highway to nowhere with the bridge out, oblivious to warning signs they should have seen. Consequently, I asked James to wait in another room while I talked first with his parents. "So, let's talk about your relationship as husband and wife first," I said.

Their body language showed that they were a little miffed by my focusing first on them. I could tell they wanted to get on with the job of correcting James' behavior.

When I minister to families in crisis, I often approach the family dynamic with a simple premise in mind: good parents produce good kids and bad parents produce troubled children. I understand that this isn't an inviolable rule. There are exceptions where truly good parents have a kid who gets misdirected as with the Prodigal Son. Stuff happens. After all, Proverbs 22:6 says, "Train up a child in the way he should go, and when he is *OLD* he will not depart from it." My emphasis on the "old" presupposes that certain children will stray but return to the fold at some later point.

But quoting that verse would be small comfort to the Smiths now. They were desperate for their son to be fixed. But just a few minutes into my dialogue with mom and dad revealed that the whole family system was sick, just as I had suspected. I first compiled some family history. Bruce and Jennifer had met at a Christian college. Both were on a career path for full-time ministry. That plan got interrupted by marriage and pregnancy. A little probing revealed that James' conception preceded marriage, something few people knew. Certainly not their church family. That bit of discomfort was a warm-up for my next line of questions.

- How much personal Bruce–Jennifer time do you two have together? "Not much."

- When did the family last get away for a vacation with just the three of them? "About four years ago. Things have been too busy."

- Do you know who James' closest friends are, and do they ever come over to the house? "We're not sure. We could ask him. He's mentioned a couple of names."

- When do you pray together as a family? "Every meal, special occasions."

- Have you ever broken family curses? "We have your book *Curse Breaking* and plan to do it sometime, but we both put in long hours and we haven't gotten to it yet."

- How often do you engage in personal intimacy and have sex? "What has that got to do with anything?"— OK, they didn't say that, but they were certainly thinking it. They emotionally stiffened with non-verbal resistance to that line of questioning.

The tension in the room was thick as a San Francisco fog. It was palpable. Both squirmed. They were so nonplussed that the long silence didn't end until I said, "Just approximate it. I don't need a log of your intimacy, just a general idea."

They glanced at each other nervously. "Uh, I don't know. A while," Bruce responded.

"What's 'a while'?"

Jennifer jumped in. "We haven't slept together in five years, if that's what you want to know."

"Separate bedrooms?"

"Not exactly. We have a pull-out couch in our bedroom and..." Jennifer forced back a tear.

"I sleep there," Bruce interjected, a tinge of anger and hurt in his voice.

"And you think that James isn't aware of that, and it has no influence on his behavior?'

"I guess we just thought that was private and none of his business," Bruce shot back.

Such was the beginning of what became an intense time of marriage intervention. But before going on with that, let me jump to the reason we're starting this book with the example of a publicly vibrant Christian couple who secretly were headed nowhere in their relationship.

CHRISTIAN FAMILIES IN CRISIS

The crisis condition of the North American, Christian family is a point that Laura and I want to make early on in this book. Far too many homes of evangelical faith are damaged and dysfunctional. After decades of counseling hundreds of couples, I have concluded that the majority—you read right—the majority of Christian families are relationally, sexually, emotionally, and spiritually out-of-sync with the message of Christ's Gospel. These families are in serious spiritual bondage and need to be set free!

Sadly, most Christian couples don't know their marriages and families are messed up and that only drastic spiritual intervention will avoid disaster. They are almost willingly ignorant of the many ways that Satan has robbed their joys and destinies. Tragically, some don't want to know how bad thing are. It's too painful to be honest about the inconsistencies between Christian values and what goes on behind closed doors.

In response to this crisis, Laura and I offer many years of experience in parenting, counseling, and ministry, including deliverance ministry. We want to emphasize at the start of this book that there is a biblical way out of the Bruce and Jennifer dilemma. But we must first acknowledge that all too many Christian families are filled with good intentions and a lot of self-deception.

LAURA'S TAKE ON PURPOSEFUL PARENTING

What Jennifer and Bruce may have missed, in all of their attempts to faithfully serve the Lord, is that God really does have a plan for parents and their children. That plan, a paradigm for all followers of Christ, is expressed in Jeremiah 29:11 (NIV): " 'For I know the plans I have for you,' declares the Lord, 'plans to prosper you and not to harm you, plans to give you hope and a future.'"

But memorizing or quoting that Scripture isn't enough. Having it cross-stitched on a sampler somewhere won't mend a broken marriage. It's easy to believe Jeremiah's words when things are going well. Maybe not so when a family crisis arises.

Let's begin with a simple premise that is foundational when Bob and I minister to a troubled family: Every one of us was created for a reason, a purpose. The trap Satan sets is getting us to think that we should be doing more. And more. And enough is never enough. This deception gets magnified when we look at our children. We know that God has a plan for them, but what if it isn't unfolding as we had imagined?

Face it. There are times when children are defiant, even rebellious. They seem to set themselves up for a questionable, even a failure-filled future. As parents, that makes us feel helpless. We ask ourselves how this could happen. They were loved and brought up with Christ's teachings from an early age. We lament over and over, "Where did we go wrong?"

Like Bruce and Jennifer in Bob's account above, too many parents are busy doing stuff, even for the Lord, and not communicating clearly to their children how to seek the will of God. It's tough to do that in the face of media portrayals of parents as clueless and out of touch. Parents have to show their children how to seek God's plan for their lives. It's obvious that the Smiths didn't do that. Grace over lunch and busyness for Jesus doesn't cut it in our age of so many immoral options.

Purposeful parenting gives the kind of guidance that lets children know they are in a spiritual battle. At times it will seem as if everything around them opposes God's will. They must know that to yield to ungodly plans for their lives is a terrible option. In fact, it is downright dangerous and can steal their eternal destiny. Purposeful parents inform their children early on that the charade of evil has been meticulously designed by the Architect of Evil himself.

If you feel challenged by your lack of parenting skills, don't hyperventilate. And don't get caught in the guilt of your past errors that drive you to insist on perfection from your children. Keep this book in hand, relax in the Lord, and let Bob and I walk you through the life lessons we've learned from personal experience and from assisting other parents with families that are out of sync. Read carefully what Bob writes next. You may find yourself on the pages that follow.

Righting the Smith's Sinking Ship

By the time that Jennifer and Bruce calmed down from their shock, I suggested a bit of musical chairs. I sent mom and dad into another room and focused on James to get his side of the story.

Not to my surprise, James' view of family life in the Smith household was far more cynical than his parents might have suspected. And his personal life was way more off course than the worst fears his parents could have imagined.

"Let's get real," I said, to start the dialogue with James. "Your parents say you're rebellious. What does that mean? Be blunt. If you don't tell the truth, I can't help you."

James hung his head to ward off a little self-consciousness and a whole lot of shame. He began talking about things his parents didn't know about him. His behavior, as self-described, had enough sin and moral inconsistencies to match someone twice his age. Drugs, sexual activity, a girlfriend on her second abortion, friends who dabbled in the occult had all been obscured from mom and dad by carefully crafted lies. James was part of the family conspiracy of hypocrisy that had been implicitly designed to keep the truth hidden so that the "perfect" Christian family image was intact.

Outward respectability and inward inconsistencies. James played the game almost as well as his parents, with their "couch in the bedroom" approach to intimate connection. James had been lying to his parents, because their lives were a lie to him. And Satan and his demons were all too pleased to nudge along this fanciful concept of Christian family life.

Then James dropped a bombshell. He had taken someone's car for a joyride, and the police had caught him just a few miles into the drive. A compassionate cop helped him return the car safely and agreed not to file a report so long as James stayed out of trouble. The incident had scared him to his core. It was enough of a close call to get his attention about the state of spiritual decline in his life. That part of his wake-up call was positive. But what James couldn't understand was how his family life had set him up for his brief criminal escapade.

I explained to James a core belief that I've adopted after decades of helping to free families. No act of defiance or rebellion exists in a vacuum of unintended consequences. All spiritual declension is the result of a family-bloodline, chain reaction. I further explained that the spiritual inconsistencies of his parents were compromising his ability to stay on the path toward godly success.

For now, let's step back, for a moment, from the Bruce/Jennifer/ James saga and consider some of the impediments that keep families from being free. I'll lay these out in a series of false assumptions that pervade the thinking of many families in crisis.

FALSE ASSUMPTIONS OF COUPLES IN CRISIS

We'll fix this ourselves. This is perhaps the most common false conclusion that I encounter when trying to help parents and children toward a more spiritually healthy way of living. This assumption enforces secrecy about even the most corrupt of conditions. It's based on the idea that devout spiritual faith gives all the information and practical tools to get out of difficult situations. Not true. A strong confidence in God and His Word is a great help to navigate the challenges that life presents. But family and parenting has its own unique, combustible mixture of destabilizing factors that can't always be reduced to a Bible verse.

A glaring fault of the "we'll fix it" syndrome is the failure to recognize that few families possess the internal objectivity to see what's wrong and take appropriate action. It's the old "can't see the forest for the trees" maxim at work. Marriage and parenting may be the most intensely, emotionally draining task to which we human beings are called. When all isn't going well it's hard to keep focused and balanced. To ask a couple to be absolutely honest about their marriage difficulties or to be transparent concerning the actions of their children may require an honesty that is nearly impossible to achieve.

By law and ethics, therapists can't treat their own families. Doctors can't diagnose and prescribe medications for spouses and children. There are good reasons for these guidelines. When an individual is too close to you, as in a family bond, impartiality with regard to good judgment may be lacking.

For the family in crisis, outside intervention is almost always necessary. You'll hear us repeat this theme over and over in this book. If the reader has a stressed marriage, if all isn't well with the parent–child relationship, get help outside the immediate family. When possible get professional help. Pastoral help. The input of trusted, mature friends. Read good "how-to" books on the various challenges of marriage and parenting. There are a lot of great books out there. Check out the book-stand of your local Christian bookstore, and you may be amazed at the quantity of information already available. Don't reinvent the wheel. Chances are that some good Christian writer already has it rolling.

Biblically instilled values will always produce the desired results in the family. Wrong again. Of course, it's good to inculcate the Word of God into the belief system of the family. But doing so is not an automatic guarantee that each member will live consistent with that teaching. Each family member has his or her own will, and they may not make individual choices that are consistent with Christian faith. "The family that prays together stays together," goes the old adage. It's mostly true, but not always.

The intense pressures of the world around us cause spiritual erosion over time. Christian kids can be caught sexting. Not every movie your children see will be OK, no matter how diligently you check the ratings and read the reviews. Music with anti-Christian lyrics, television shows with off-color themes, and profane comments from supposedly Christian peers may all take a toll on your children. Teaching them what God says will help deter them from making bad choices, but don't assume that consistent godliness will be the automatic result of having a Christ-centered home. Raising your children with godly principles will give them an advantage in life, but it won't ensure that all their choices will be healthy ones.

Providing a good Christian education will keep children on the right path. Not necessarily so. Laura and I are certainly in favor of having children attend a Christian school or having them homeschooled, so long as finances and circumstances allow. We have homeschooled all three of our daughters. I say "we," but I'll be the first to admit that Laura has borne the main responsibility of their education because of my work and travel schedule. Laura has done an amazing job, but it has been extraordinarily stressful and demanding; however, there hasn't been a moment when we've regretted making the decision to homeschool our children. Scholastically and spiritually they are way ahead of most of their secular, public-schooled contemporaries. The sacrifices our family has made to pursue this educational direction has been worth it. But we realize that this option isn't always possible for all families, especially single parents.

Even though we extol the value of Christian schools and homeschooling, we have observed many families that took that direction and ended up with far less than desired results. As you might imagine, there are many reasons that this choice of education didn't work out as hoped. We'll not dissect, at this point, all the factors of failure. Just be aware that there are no guarantees that a Christian education will be the best. However, Laura and I are convinced that, given the moral and scholastic conditions of most public schools, your parental chances for success with your children are a lot better if school courses are taught in the framework of Christian values.

If we keep our children in church, things will turn out OK. Regular church attendance will help. It's the biblical thing to do. It provides regular communication of God's Word. There are better opportunities for friendships with Christian friends. If there's a good youth group, your children will be more occupied with activities that are morally healthy. The length of benefits from a healthy church relationship are almost endless. But a strong church relationship isn't a fix-all for what may be wrong at home.

Over and over, Christian kids in trouble tell me that the advantages they got from exposure to Christian faith in church didn't outweigh the damage of a home where Christ was not Lord in any practical sense. Hypocrisy in the home is a huge reason why many youth don't follow the faith of their fathers. They don't want what Mom and Dad had, because it didn't work in real life, at least not as they observed it with their parents. In homes where church attendance was mandatory every week, kids who have gone wrong have told me:

- "Sure, my parents took us to church, but at home we never talked. I never felt close to them. They never said they loved me."

- "Mom and Dad behaved perfectly at church, but at home they fought all the time. It was miserable being around them because they were always ready to blow up at each other."

- "At church, there was all this hugging and hand-shaking, but at home my parents never showed any affection to each other except occasionally. I don't even know if they were in love with each other."

- "Mom and Dad were hypocrites. They acted at home a lot different from the way they did in church. If that's Christianity, I don't want it."

- "I don't even know what I believe. I hear what the preacher says, but it doesn't seem to work for our family. I just wish my parents would act like what they hear on Sunday."

The theme is common. Hypocrisy, inconsistency, disingenuousness, phoniness. Children quickly see through the claims of "freedom in Jesus" on Sunday and bondage to bad habits and variant behavior six days a week at home.

We need to stay together for the sake of the children. No, you don't. I'm not suggesting you immediately call a divorce lawyer. I am aware that many pastors think a bad marriage with a two-parent home is better for a child than a broken home. I'm not so sure. I've seen many instances demonstrating the consequences of both sides of this kind of situation. My own counseling experience indicates that when parents stay together in an acrimonious relationship, the effect this has on children is often more damaging than a divorce. Deciding which is best may mean choosing the proverbial "lesser of two evils."

Divorce can be devastating to a child. But a conflict-ridden marriage may be more damaging. Today in America, about 25 percent of children will end up in a stepfamily. At least a million children a year suffer through a divorce. Witnessing the loss of love in a home and then being shuttled back and forth between divorced parents can be a defining trauma in the life of a child. Their sense of trust is shaken, especially when the youngster sees the parents fighting over custody and behaving in very undependable ways. This may result in the child fancifully longing for a parental reunion. Without some solid Christian influence in such a situation, the separation anxiety can result in a permanent condition of instability.

But when the parents only cohabit for the benefit of the children, there can be equally devastating consequences. Such children often become depressed, even suicidal. During adolescence, the child of a bad marriage may be prone to drug or alcohol abuse and self-injurious behavior. Once grown they may be hindered when trying to process stress and anger. Their resiliency to handle life's challenges will be severely restricted. Of course, a confident spiritual faith can override all these negatives. But a gloomy outcome in life is going to be hard to avoid. I want to underscore that both divorce and a phony marriage in the "best interests" of the child are equally bad. And neither should have to happen if both parents will determine to set the family free with the right kind of help.

We're Christians, we don't believe in divorce, so somehow it will all work out. How many times have I heard that? Countless. How many times have I seen that go south? Countless. These are the same couples who don't seek counseling, or at least one of the partners refuses to. Why?

Here is their logic. They're going to pray their way through it. They're trusting Jesus to heal their marriage. God can move mountains, why not mend their marriage? Besides, if they go to counseling, someone will find out that the family isn't as perfect as it appears. That will be embarrassing and raise a lot of questions they'd prefer not to answer.

Let me bluntly tell you that this is a surefire setup for an affair, if not physical, at least emotional. Very few couples can continue in a loveless marriage, especially when it is sexless. Yes, "for the sake of the children" some survive for a while, but things usually fall apart when the kids are gone. The couple that refuses to get help for a struggling marriage is allowing Satan to position them for an even worse outcome—a moral fiasco. The marriage partner whose emotional and physical needs aren't being met at home is giving the devil an open door to send along some who will commiserate with their dilemma. In fact, if your marriage is on the rocks or nearing the shoals of failure, Satan may already have someone picked out to seductively cross your path. And because failing to forthrightly address the marriage crisis is a transgression against the marriage, a demonic door is open. I've seen this scenario too many times.

"But I'd never do that," some say. To counter, we could cite the names of many well-known and successful evangelical pastors who have morally fallen in recent years. They were spiritually gifted. They built large and successful mega-churches. They wrote best-selling books and were on TV telling others how to live. Some even came from a lineage of godly predecessors in their family. The list of such men is a long, tragic commentary on the state of marriage in America. I have counseled some of these men and their wives. Some even resorted to pornography to jump start the marriage bed. Others turned to alcohol and illegal drugs. One well-known pastor of a huge international church admitted to having sex with forty or fifty women in his church. The number wasn't precise because he couldn't remember all of them!

The ones that I have ministered to all tell me that they never saw themselves ending up spiritually shipwrecked. In the words of one famous pastor who eventually divorced, "I didn't know there was anything wrong with my marriage." Really? Was he that clueless? Likely.

How can that be? Couples in crisis sometimes normalize their marital contradictions. They lie to themselves. They think that by hanging in there, God will somehow perform a miracle and rescue them. They have several things in common. They can never think of themselves as divorcing. They assume that their faith will keep them from sexual sin. They convince themselves that a bad marriage is their cross to bear for Jesus.

The list of personal prevarications embraced by Christian leaders with bad marriages is lengthy. But all the self-deception leads to tragic places: a dingy hotel room and paid sex with a prostitute; self-medication with addictive substances; unquenchable anger at their mate and sometimes at God, to name a few bad possibilities. Don't think it can't happen to you, because it can! Were it not for sworn confidentiality, I could tell you of names you'd know, of men and women of God who lived the kind of lies that I've just cited. Many of them lost their ministries, their reputations, their self-respect, even their families.

For heaven's sake, if you're reading this book providentially and you see yourself on these pages, pick up your phone and call someone you can trust. Or make contact with a counseling professional who specializes in marriage intervention. Contact our offices and set up a personal meeting with me to talk about your issues. We can help. Others can help. But you probably can't help yourself.

Seeking help can be the sign of a *good* marriage. Laura and I will let you in on a secret. We've been to counseling for our marriage. First, before we got married we sought advice from a mature Christian advisor. We'll allude to this individual later in the book. This Christian leader had written books on marriage. We read his books and met with him for premarriage evaluation. Second, soon after we were married we sought further counseling to work out the wrinkles that any newly married couple will have. We didn't seek help because we were in crisis. We didn't have a bad marriage. We reached out because we wanted a better marriage. We needed objective input to work through some challenges we encountered during the adjustment to married life and starting our family.

Please don't miss this important point. I'm repeating it for emphasis. We didn't seek help for a dysfunctional marriage, we sought professional advice to make our marriage stronger.

Many churches see the need for pre marriage counseling, although such arrangements are often only a cursory sign-off for the wedding ceremony. But there are some excellent programs to get couples started right. If you are thinking of getting married, be certain that the church in which your nuptials will take place has such requirements. This is an indication that the church and pastor take your wedding vows seriously.

Here's my concern. I don't know of churches that also require a marriage check-up *after* the couple is wedded. In some ways, that's when intervention is most needed. After the honeymoon period, when the couple is thinking of getting pregnant or when the first serious conflicts arise—that is when further evaluation is needed. Setting the family free shouldn't start when there is a calamity like Bruce and Jennifer's, fifteen to twenty years into the marriage.

Laura and I spend a lot of time trying to patch together the broken lives of couples who are on the verge of separation or divorce. We also help couples who reach out for help at the first sign of serious conflict. The latter is much easier to fix than the former. To be certain that no reader is missing the point, let me lay it out clearly:

1. Competent premarriage counseling is a must to get the marriage started well.

2. Post marriage counseling, preferably within the first year following the wedding, is a good way to checkup on the health of the developing marriage bond.

3. Marriage accountability to a pastor or wise spiritual advisors is important throughout married life to constantly reflect on areas needing improvement.

4. At the first sign of serious marital difficulties, adept outside help should be sought through books, seminars, enrichment programs, and whatever resources are readily available.

5. Adding children to the marriage equation is an important time for marriage reevaluation. The stresses on a marriage can be much more than most couples realize.

A Happy Ending for Bruce, Jennifer, and James

I wish I could say that, with the help of Christ, our ministry has been able to save every bad marriage that has come our way. That's not so. But we were able to get the Smith family back on track. It took some serious prodding to make Bruce realize his failures as a father and husband. A lot of healing prayer was needed to allow Jennifer to forgive and attempt a new start for the relationship. And it was very difficult to turn around James' cynicism and sense of despair about his future. But I'm happy to report today that the Smiths are well on the road to recovery. They are becoming a testimony to grace, not another statistic of failure.

It required many hours of therapeutic interaction between all three family members, with me interceding as an arbiter to enforce family honesty. It took repentance, reconciliation, and a lot of healing and deliverance prayers to move things closer to a biblical family model. One session didn't do it. We had to meet and pray several times. Each person had spiritual and relational homework to do. But over time, a true Christian marriage evolved and James was able to stabilize his connection to both parents.

Divorce was avoided and James came to realize that his parents truly loved each other. He saw that love restored. Bruce and Jennifer now spend a lot more time together, and they have reunited on an intimate level. All is good for now, but I have been careful to warn this family that Satan waits at the door of their home, looking for permission to get back inside. Their family has set free, but now they need to learn how to live free and stay free!

Chapter Two

TWO TO TANGO

It's not unusual for Laura and me to counsel a wife or husband and discover, before we're too far into the session, that there's a critical element missing. The spouse who shows up for our time together pours out his or her heart, sometimes with intense emotion. A long list of grievances, catalogued over time, rush forth in a torrent. The one partner who is seeking help has waited a long time to find someone who will listen empathetically, and we're the first ones to whom they've exposed their soul.

As the supplicant proceeds, Laura and I often share a knowing glance with a complimentary thought in mind: "We can't properly help this person because only half of the equation of pain and dysfunction is present." It takes two to tango and only one is on the dance floor.

INEQUITABLE RELATIONSHIPS

That's the way it was with Rick and Rose. Rose knew that Rick had serious spiritual issues, perhaps even demons, hence her interest in having Rick see me. But at the appointed time for Rick's session, only Rose walked into the room. It was obvious she was in a dejected state.

"Rick refused to come," she explained. "Ironically, it was his idea in the first place. He's followed your ministry for years, and has even talked about enrolling in your online School of Exorcism. But when it came time to leave for the appointment, he said he had too much work to do."

I calmed Rose down as well as I could, assuring her that I'd seen this same pattern before. One spouse initiates the idea of getting help, only to back out belatedly.

"I always see that as the opportunity for God to do something for the one who does show up," I consoled Rose. "Perhaps, somehow, this is what God wanted. Maybe you're the one who needs deliverance."

Rose looked at me in shock. "I'm OK," she responded. "Rick's the one with the anger and relationship issues. It's tearing our marriage apart. I don't know how much longer I can take it."

I allowed her to vent her frustrations a little, and then interjected, "Let's take this situation as it is, and see it as an opportunity for you to heal."

That was all right with her. She just didn't want to hear any talk about her needing prayer for any serous spiritual oppression. So, I began by letting her express all the accumulated frustration from a seventeen-year marriage that had started out well but was now in danger of crashing.

"I've thought a lot about leaving Rick," she admitted. "I'd probably do it tomorrow if it wasn't for the kids...and the shame of ruining our Christian witness."

After decades of hearing stories like this I've learned to listen beyond the words being spoken. To look past the obvious and detect deeper spiritual signals. It was becoming apparent to me that in spite of what need there was for Rick to have deliverance, the most immediate necessity for prayer was right in front of us.

Not only was Rick missing, so were the children. All too often in situations like this, the children are collateral damage. The parents are so focused on their own issues with each other that the kids are kicked to the curb. Not intentionally. In most cases, parents would insist they love their children and want the best for them. But in the emotional cauldron of a dying or dysfunctional marriage, all the partners can often see is their own pain.

"So," I said, "if you are hanging in there for the kids, tell me about them?"

"We have two. Jessica—she's twelve, and moody, depressed—and Johnathan—he's our oldest—scares me the most. He plays in a band. Plays at church too, but I think his real love is the metal music of his unsaved friends. He seems to be under some kind of spell. Him and his girlfriend both. Maybe it's the drugs or something." Rose sobbed. "It's just...just too much for me."

Rose broke down into a full-blown emotional collapse, crying and shaking with little control. Her life was unraveling. Satan was picking off each family member one by one. But for now, the only place we could start was with Rose. At this stage, she was the only willing party.

That day, Rick being absent, Rose experienced a deliverance from Satan that might not have taken place had Rick been there. Although I couldn't resolve the conflicts of the marriage, by God's grace Rose was able to deal with her issues. Had Rick been by her side, she might have been too focused on her anger toward him, which could have obscured the ancestral bondage that she suffered.

Rose described the pattern of occult events in her life. Her mother practiced witchcraft and her grandmother was a high-level witch. It was common for her as a child to find raw eggs in her bedroom, put there by her mother as "protection" against evil spirits. Grandma had the ability to move objects to demonstrate her power. In addition to this, a brother had molested her as a child. When all the levels of evil had been peeled back, we discovered a twenty-generation curse going back to her

Mexican, Aztec ancestors who had worshipped the feathered serpent god, Quetzalcoatl (aka Lucifer), a common demon found in those of Hispanic ancestry. The curses were broken, and Rose was set free.

But what about her family? Here's the good news. A month later, Rose scheduled another Personal Encounter session with me. This time Rick was there.

Like Rose, Rick had a troubled life. He described growing up in a neighborhood of gangs, where it was almost kill or be killed. His father beat his mother, and he too had been molested as a child. As his story of misery unfolded, I noticed a tattoo peeking out from under his left shirtsleeve.

I felt impressed by the Lord to ask, "What's that? Do you mind showing me?"

Rick rolled up his sleeve to reveal the huge tattoo of an Indian warrior, with a large headdress and a skull for a face.

"Where I lived as a kid was so violent that I got this to show how tough I was, to scare people."

I dipped my finger into holy anointing oil and placed the sign of the cross over this hideous body art. When I did, a growl came from deep inside Rick. As the demonic manifestation took over, I demanded to know what demon was tormenting Rick, and trying to destroy his family. The answer was unsurprising.

"Quetzalcoatl. We don't have his wife anymore, but we still have this man."

The outcome to this demonic encounter with Rick was the same as with Rose. Rick followed me in repeating curse-breaking prayers, and this ancient Aztec demon met the same judgment as his evil partner who had inhabited Rose's bloodline.

Once the demons were gone from Rose, and now Rick, we addressed the marriage issues, without interference from the generational evil spirits. The key to setting this family free was deliverance from demonic intrusion and having both spouses present to honestly face their differences.

But this success story isn't necessarily typical. The failure to have both spouses agree to seek help is only one of many challenges faced by those who seek to help couples in marital predicaments. Once you've read the next section you'll see why it is so important to have both marriage partners participate in setting the family free.

THE FAMILY ASSIGNMENTS OF SATAN

Marriage and family difficulties usually fall into one of several categories. To set a family at liberty, it's helpful to know which of these classifications predominates. In most cases, a family in plight may fit into more than one bracket. But one usually prevails as being the most important to correct. The reader might be surprised that the list is so long. It could have been much longer, but we elected to group several disputations under a single heading.

This is not a marriage counseling book, and thus our intent is not to exhaustively examine the causes and solutions for each of these troubles. Instead, this list serves several purposes. First, it gives the reader an idea of what our own experience has been in helping families that aren't doing well. Second, it shows the depth of difficulties faced by many families in today's world. Each of the twenty problems that families face deserves its own chapter, or perhaps its own book. But a short survey of each will give those reading this book a point of comparison with the strains on their family structure.

Because my primary calling is that of an exorcist and the focus of our ministry is on inner healing and deliverance, a legitimate question might be, "Where does this list fit into the template of understanding Satan's assignments on the family?"

The devil attacks the human condition in three basic ways: (1) he initiates an assault and creates a problem, (2) he exploits a pre existing condition, or (3) he uses some combination of these two tactics.

Take, for example, number seven on this list—offensive habits. On the surface, this issue doesn't seem like something that would sink a marriage, but think more about how Satan can exploit such a situation. He may influence one of the marriage partners to start doing something that their spouse finds annoying. Then the devil works on that disagreement to stoke the fires of dissention. Or, Satan may be aware of some area of behavior that a person's spouse won't like. (Don't underestimate the meticulousness of the devil's machinations. Even I, an experienced deliverance minister, am constantly astounded at the intricacies of demonic manipulation to achieve some evil end.) Once Satan senses one of the marriage partners is offended with even the smallest feelings of disgust, irritation, and disharmony, he goes to work. The devil may place a demon on assignment to focus on this one area of potential marriage disruption.

This is not to say that every contention in a family structure is the work of the devil. Satan is a lazy creature because of his fallen, corrupt nature. He won't expend energy to unravel something that will break down of its accord. But if demonic forces deem it necessary to intervene in some family issue to bring any kind of hurt or harm, they won't hesitate a moment to be actively engaged in disruption and dissention.

Will just any demon do, if there is an assignment of Satan? No. Evil has a hierarchy. My book, *Demon Proofing Prayers* explains at length how this operates. The teaching in our International School of Exorcism has several courses designed to reveal how the infernal structure of evil functions. Satan's kingdom is well-organized with a militaristic matrix of intricacy and coordination. My book *Jezebel: Defeating Your #1 Spiritual Enemy* describes some ways that the evil spirit Jezebel destroys families. Demons that commonly accompany Jezebel on this mission are Lust, Rejection, Contention, Unforgiveness, Anger, Rage, Abuse, Offense, and Adultery. If your family is under spiritual attack, this is one place to start directing your prayers.

Some readers who aren't as up to speed in their understanding of spiritual warfare might look a little askance at what I've just written. It's not common in most evangelical churches to talk about the devil, and less so to address the topic of direct, demonic activity. It's even more rare to bring up the idea that individual demons with specific names and detailed instructions from Hell might be targeting a particular family.

If this is a bit too much to grasp, think of Paul's words in 2 Corinthians 12:7. The apostle declared that devil had assigned a specific demon to torment him. Most Bible translations are consistent regarding this reference. The New International Version says "messenger of Satan" as does both New King James Version, King James Version, New American Standard Version, and the Amplified Version. That's an unusual consistency for such a controversial text.

What do Bible commentators say? Matthew Henry suggested it was "some great trouble or some great temptation" or "acute bodily pain or sickness." Albert Barnes wrote, "In the time of the Saviour malignant spirits are known to have taken possession of the body in numerous cases, and to have produced painful bodily diseases, and Paul here says that Satan was permitted to bring this calamity on him." It's disingenuous of preachers and theologians to explain this verse away by saying it was anything other than a demonic attack, simply because they want to avoid a hardcore approach to dealing with demons. But the language of Scripture is very specific when it says "a messenger of Satan." An evil spirit was "on assignment" to attack Paul.

If Christians believe that the family is the bedrock foundation of civilization and the most important bulwark against cultural and moral disintegration, is it so hard to imagine that there are specific demons directed by the devil to destroy homes and marriages, including your family?

Twenty Areas Where Satan Attacks the Family

Let me first list what Laura and I believe are the top twenty ways that the devil tries to destroy marriages and the family. I'll add a few comments about each to help the reader better understand why families need to be free from these attacks.

1. **An uncooperative husband or wife:** Why is this at the top of the list? It is the easiest way that Satan can impede a couple from getting help, as in the case of Rick and Rose above. Few cases of family discord are one-sided; therefore, it's hard to render an adequate evaluation of relationship differences if you're only hearing from one of the mates. Lack of cooperation is a roadblock that's almost impossible to surpass. One of the partners may get counseling or receive prayer assistance, but that still leaves the seeking spouse stuck in an irresolute condition. He or she may be working hard to heal the family, but marriage, as we consistently point out, is a "one-flesh" relationship. Seeking resolution for family problems by talking to only the husband or wife is like having a broken leg in your body and expecting it to function normally just because the rest of the body is healthy.

2. **Health challenges:** If any evil spirit of infirmity is involved, the suffering family may have to battle on two fronts: the bodily and the spiritual. The stress caused by a major health challenge can severely affect the family. Schedules may be disrupted. Finances are usually strained. Employment may be difficult to maintain if constant care is needed. Marital intimacy is sometimes affected. The emotional toll may eventually outweigh the physical strain.

3. **Insecurity and rejection issues:** We emphasize several places in this book how important it is to come into a marriage with as clean a slate as possible. Emotional baggage from the past from either spouse can poison the entire family. If rejection issues, for example, plagued the mother or father before marriage, these problems won't go away after the wedding. Some enter marriage with the idea that love is going to heal their wounds. In most cases, that is not so. In fact, the inevitable conflicts of married life usually make past emotional problems worse. The spouse with a demonic stronghold of rejection will find that marriage disagreements feed the fire of emotional repudiation even more.

4. **Children in rebellion:** When adolescent, emotional adjustments turn into full-blown rebellion, the entire family is contaminated. Siblings can be affected, as they try to remain emotionally grounded

while a brother or sister spins out of control. Mom and Dad are focused on damage control, trying to find the source of the revolt and keeping it contained. Remember that 1 Samuel 15:23 states that rebellion is like the sin of witchcraft. What the family faces may be post pubescent adjustments and growing pains; however, it can also become a raging spiritual fire fueled by evil spirits of Jezebel and witchcraft with an assignment to destroy the home.

5. **Unrealistic expectations:** Almost all couples enter marriage a little starry-eyed. That's love. But if there is no premarital counseling process, as so strongly recommended in this book, there might be little objectivity to balance the newlyweds. Without open and honest discussions concerning the very real provocations that married life brings, one of the spouses could quickly fall into depression or anger, or both. Every family unit has limitations, whether they are financial, emotional, or educational. Advance thinking before marriage about these constraints will help to offset one of the spouses from raising the bar of marital expectations too high, presenting their partner with an almost impossible goal to reach in the relationship.

6. **Busyness with life's demands:** Married life has a way of becoming exponentially more complicated as the years go by. Children, employment, financial obligations, meshing of in-laws, finding mutual friends, changing career opportunities—all affect the ability to keep intimacy alive in a marriage. Henry David Thoreau observed, "It is not enough to be busy; so are the ants. The question is: what are we busy about?" Christ told us to consider the lilies of the field as they effortlessly grow without excessive concern. Sustaining all that is required for a modern family to function can be an overwhelming endeavor. In time, mental clutter, overscheduling, and physical fatigue can lead to depression and emotional inertia. If couples aren't careful, conversations become shorter and shorter, sex less frequent, church attendance more optional, and the things that drew them together are forgotten, or at least minimized. Laura and I encourage couples who are overcome with the hectic pace of life to spend more time together talking about the

things that created attraction in the first place. What were mutual interests? What activities did both enjoy doing? What spiritual concerns did they share in the beginning? Our advice is simple: Set your marriage free by getting back to the basics of what drew you together in the first place.

7. **Offensive habits:** This is one of those topics that few couples want to bring up, as we mentioned earlier. It might be embarrassing to discuss the personal hygiene of one's spouse. The coupling of a perfectionist "neatie" to an unrepentant "messy" may cause unspoken resentment if not voiced and worked through. Offense can be taken to snoring, burping, sneezing, and...well use your imagination about all the bodily functions that should be disciplined when you are living with someone in close proximity. This may not seem to be a very spiritual thing to talk about, but Satan will use anything at his disposal that creates disharmony and internalized anger. Once again, this is where a counselor can be a mediator to broach delicate subjects, without either spouse having to approach the other in an accusatory manner that could hurt or cause an unforgiving attitude.

8. **Inadequate or flawed communication:** Lack of verbal adeptness or listening skills is high on the list of marriage deal-breakers, especially with women. In our Marriage Encounters we walk couples through seven levels of communication, ranging from "casual conversation" to "intimate engagement." It would be too lengthy here to discuss all that we explain while encouraging couples to higher levels of communication, but we basically describe an ascending degree of connection that moves from the nonintimate to intimate soul-sharing. This isn't something that most couples in crisis can work out on their own. A skilled negotiator in marriage communication is helpful. The reality is that, if a couple isn't talking to each other at a needed level of intimacy, more talking by the same couple will likely make things worse. The more they try to communicate, which they aren't very good at anyway, they will likely make the same mistakes over and over. Some couples become highly skilled at defaulting to arguments. It's what they do, and

over time, such behavior becomes normalized. More of the same will probably make the relationship worse, not better.

9. **Baggage from prior marriages or relationships:** This is another touchy subject. The essential question is how much and what is taboo to talk about and what boundaries are established early on in the marriage? Every couple will handle this differently, depending on the relevancy of the information. For example, it probably isn't helpful to discuss the sexual habits of a prior partner, but it may be important to openly talk about things that can affect the new partnership. Examples would be: (1) Prior domestic violence that might arouse fears of being hurt when the new partner gets angry, (2) demeaning language by the prior partner that can trigger feelings of rejection if the current spouse speaks harshly or without proper thought, (3) negative patterns of spiritual behavior that may raise fears if the new partner acts in less than a godly way. Common sense is in order with this area of relationship management. The general rule is this: If you don't need to tell it, then leave it in the past; if it can affect the new relationship by resurrecting old hurts or fears, then get those issues into the open.

10. **Division of responsibilities:** In the newness of a marriage, this may seem like a little thing. But as the marriage goes on, failure of one spouse to assist the other can become a big issue. For example: You have to hound him to take out the trash; you have to constantly remind her to not leave the oven on; you have to make sure he's put the toilet seat down when it's late at night and dark; you need her cooperation to treat nonessential expenses with prudence and not overcharge the credit card. These challenges are best met with open, frank, ongoing discussions that are polite and not personally defamatory. In these cases, try to avoid the word "you," as in "you did this" or "you didn't do that." Focus on the problem the situation creates, not the failures of the person who caused the problem. Over time, most couples implicitly negotiate a division of labor and accountability. If that isn't done quite naturally, then intervention may be in order before deep indignation results.

11. **Strained conflict resolution:** From governments navigating international affairs to newlyweds embarking on shared goals, it's important to know how to, and how not to, resolve conflicts. Our Marriage Encounters teach couples to do this in constructive ways. Here are a few key tips that will aid in dialing down the level of conflict when differences are encountered:

- Be willing to listen to the viewpoint of your spouse without counterpoint. Practice empathetic listening that genuinely hears the other side.

- Affirming an opposing person's right to speak their mind doesn't mean agreeing with their viewpoint. It does mean that you respect their integrity.

- Avoid body language that sends antagonistic signals, like nodding off (yes, some marriage partners do that), rolling one's eyes (as in "give me a break"), failing to make eye contact (we men have a real problem with this), and looking at your watch or cell phone (a sure way to escalate the argument).

- Saying "I apologize" doesn't indicate that you've conceded your position. It does mean that you feel genuinely bad that the other person is hurt, even if you do think it was their fault. (Don't say that!)

- End the discussion/confrontation with prayer. And don't pray for the Lord to show the other person where they are wrong. Genuinely meet at the Cross on the common ground that we are all sinners saved by grace, and we are all flawed creatures who are often incapable of seeing where we have personally erred.

12. **Financial pressures:** Some good books have been written about family money management. No sense reinventing the wheel here. But some basic advice is in order. In a two-income family, will resources be shared with equal access? Will you and your spouse have joint or

separate accounts? Will assets be held jointly or separately? How will the annual IRS return be filed? What if parents or in-laws need financial assistance? How much debt will be incurred? What policies will be adhered to regarding the use of credit cards and revolving credit? Who will manage the checking account(s)? These aren't the only questions to ask, and there aren't necessarily right or wrong answers, but what's crucial is that things aren't left unspoken and at the mercy of the latest argument of how much was spent and what was purchased. You might ask a future partner how things were handled in their birth family, or what policies did or did not work in a prior marriage or relationship. Marriage counselors will quickly say that far too many marriages fail over matters of money or sex, and money usually trumps sex.

13. **Extended family interference:** Guess what. All those jokes about interfering in-laws aren't jokes. When two people marry, they are marrying more than each other. They are combining two legacies, two bloodlines, with all the good and bad of both. That's how the concept of arranged marriages started. Two families got together and decided if sufficient familial commonalities existed. No sense leaving such an important decision to such incompetent kids who were leading with their hearts and not with their heads. Let cooler heads prevail and do what's best for everyone. Then, along came the idea of romantic love. Romeo and Juliet. Love songs and Hollywood. Couples forgot that they were each marrying into a long line of behavioral patterns, some good and some bad. Today, in certain Asian cultures, especially where finances are limited, everyone lives under one roof. In such cases, the wife might end up cooking for his mother. You might be working for her father. In twenty-first-century America that's usually not the case, but meddling mothers-in-law and financially finicky fathers-in-law abound. Before you marry, meet the families, and not just under circumstances when all are on best behavior. Most important, know them spiritually. Christian or non-Christian? Baptist? Pentecostal? Catholic? If you understand spiritual warfare, do they? Will an in-law demand infant baptism if that's not your conviction, or vice versa? Are your in-laws old-school legalists

who will panic the first time they see you in shorts? These might seem to be irrelevant, even comical, issues, but I know of many marriages that have crashed over the silliest religious controversies. Don't give Jezebel an inch to operate in this area.

14. **An unforgiving spirit:** Forgiveness is at the heart of the Gospel. We are saved because we are forgiven (1 John 1:9). Christ forgive those who killed him (Luke 23:34). One reason that the Jewish leaders sought to destroy Jesus was because He was forgiving sinners (Luke 5:21). Forgiveness is the guiding principle of the Lord's Prayer (Matthew 6:12). We are to forgive others without limit ("seventy times seven"—Matthew 18:22). The command is clear: If we forgive others, God will forgive us (Matthew 6:14). Innumerable are the times that Laura and I have counseled a brokenhearted spouse, who says with great pain and defiance, "I will never forgive him/her!" If that statement is an ungodly vow, that marriage may be doomed. That family may never be free.

How can a spouse who is the victim of unconscionable actions ever forgive? That person must comprehend these three things: (1) forgiving is not forgetting, (2) forgiving by faith is not the same as condoning the bad behavior, and (3) living by the commands of Christ doesn't mean that indefensible, harmful behavior must be tolerated. Forgiving a spouse doesn't mean that continuing in the relationship is necessary, especially if there has been unfaithfulness or life-threatening violence.

15. **Ill-defined relationship boundaries:** Most couples that we counsel receive our recommendation to read the Dr. Henry Cloud book series on boundaries. (He has written a variety of books on this theme, but couples in crisis need to read at least his seminal work, *Boundaries*.) Violation of healthy boundaries can occur between husbands and wives, spouses and in-laws, and parents and children. Boundaries are needed to keep at a safe distance emotionally unhealthy siblings, intruding ex-spouses and lovers, unwelcome friends, theologically pushy fellow Christians, and whoever violates the sanctity of the one-flesh relationship of man and wife. To keep your family free, the devil must know

that nothing and no one will be allowed to come between you and your spouse.

16. **Emotional infidelity:** Laura and I have both been shocked to hear about the emotional affairs that are tolerated in some marriages. No husband or wife must ever have a confidant of the opposite sex to whom they share innermost feelings unless that person is a professionally qualified counselor. Allowing this level of emotional attachment is a slippery slope to other possible soul-ties, including sexual ones. "But she/he understands me in a way that my wife/husband doesn't? She/he listens and my wife/husband won't." Even if that is true, it is a violation of the marriage bond. Any married individual who feels drawn into such a triangle needs to get out fast. There may indeed be a need to unburden the soul to someone. But that someone needs to be a person who maintains a healthy and spiritually appropriate distance.

17. **Adultery:** Nearly every culture, tradition, and religion has strictures against a married partner having sex outside the marriage. In the Old Testament moral code, adultery was a capital offense. In some Muslim countries today, a woman proved to be an adulterer can be stoned. It has historically been primary grounds for divorce. Traditionally, it has been considered, after homicide, the most punishable of all crimes. Technically, in a legal sense, sexual intercourse must occur for the adultery to occur. But the standard of Christ in Matthew 5:28 raised the bar to include, "Whoever looks at a woman to lust for her has already committed adultery with her in his heart." Despite social trends toward open marriages, sexual threesomes, and polygamy, there is no biblical justification for such arrangements. More pertinent to our concerns is the bad advice giving by some pastors, who counsel an offended spouse (usually a woman) to remain in a marriage that is unrepentantly adulterous in order to save it. Some go so far as to tell the woman to keep having sex with her husband during his time of adultery with another woman. That is sheer folly. We have dealt with women who became demonized by this kind of arrangement. I've had demons reveal to me that evil spirits from the outside adulterous partner passed to the

unfaithful husband via that immoral soul-connection, then these same demons passed from the adulterous husband to his unsuspecting wife. We've also encountered wives, and husbands, who became infected with sexual diseases by an unfaithful spouse. If your spouse is indulging in adultery, get her/him out of your bed and out of your head immediately, until there can be proper spiritual intervention.

18. **Sexual and intimacy issues:** From our counseling experience, Laura and I have determined that too many in the evangelical Christian community have a hangover from times when sexual issues in marriage were never discussed. Later in the book, in the chapter, "The Facts on the Facts of Life," we'll address specific issues of certain sexual practices. Our plea at this point is to encourage Christian couples with any kind of sexual hang-ups or dysfunction to seek help immediately. Hopefully, you live in or near to a large enough metropolitan area so that you can get proper professional help. If not, drive or fly. Let nothing stop you. Our ministry offers Encounter programs to help with sexual dysfunction. If things are amiss in the bedroom, the worst thing you can do is *nothing*. Perhaps you don't even know what to ask. Don't let lack of information or embarrassment stand in your way. Here are the most common questions that come our way: (1) How frequently should sex occur? (2) What activities are wrong? (3) What if I don't like something that my spouse wants to do? You deserve sound biblical and practical answers. Chapter nine of this book will help.

19. **Unequal spiritual compatibility:** Most Christians are aware of the warning of 2 Corinthians 6:14 to not be "unequally yoked together with unbelievers." They understand that Christians should marry those of like spiritual persuasion. But suppose that your spouse seemed to be Christ-like during courtship, but you find later in marriage that it was a ruse or that he or she has grown cold in their walk with God. What then? Few marriages stay together in wedded bliss when there are significant spiritual divisions. Of course, these issues are best solved before marriage. But what if you were misled about your partner's measure of faith? Don't assume that over time things will improve without help.

Don't think that prayer without action will necessarily fix the problem. To husbands, we say, God has made you the "head" of the home (Ephesians 5:23) but that charge carries a responsibility. You must give up your life for your wife and be willing to die for her (Ephesians 5:25). The best marriages, the freest families, are ones where the husband and wife equally share God's calling for a Christian family, and both contribute accordingly to putting Christ first in the home.

20. **Demonization by one or both partners:** Now we get to our area of family specialty. If one or both spouses is demonized, the marriage is likely to be eventually doomed. Chances for success are slim without intervention. Some advice: If you are in a troubled marriage, don't read one of my books or watch me on our YouTube Exorcism Channel and try to cast demons out of your spouse. Resentment more than success will likely be the result. You may mean well, but your objectivity will be lacking. If you are inexperienced, your fix may be worse than the problem. Don't stir up demons unless you know what you're doing. And if you're wrong, labeling an oppositional spouse as having demons may be the ultimate blow to the marriage. A place to start is breaking curses. Turn to pages 145–170 in my book *Curse Breaking* and read together the prayers to renounce generational evil. Make any attempt at spiritual warfare a mutual quest for freedom. But a spouse attempting deliverance in a bad marriage situation is one of those "Don't do this at home" situations.

Chapter Three

WHY GOOD FAMILIES GO BAD

We're off and running into this book, but we need to pause and ask a few pertinent questions that the reader surely wonders about:

- What is a good family?
- What is a bad family?
- What makes a good family go bad?

Let's start with a definition of what's "good." These terms are relative, of course, but working definitions for this book will give the roadmap for where we're headed.

Good. The two families we've discussed in prior chapters were good by outside appearances. Friends, relatives, even acquaintances at church considered them models of Christian rectitude. Obviously, such opinions were based on criteria that were somewhat superficial, lacking inside information regarding what went on behind the four walls of home.

It may be too clichéd to say that "good" can be defined as regular church attendance, dedicated involvement in the activities of that church, and a smiling face every Sunday. Stand outside your local Unitarian church (a group that believes in most everything and derides nothing) and you can see similar spiritual fraudulence. We expect more of evangelical Christians than a facade, and we should. But we must stop assessing the health of a marriage and family by the brief Sunday show of piety.

Before we consider how to reorder bad families, let's look at what makes a good family. Consider these guidelines, which aren't necessarily on the list of the "evangelical seal of approval" practices. (Some of these points have already been made, but we emphasize them again here.)

1. Strong bonds of communication between husband and wife.

2. Emotional, spiritual, and sexual intimacy in the marriage.

3. Positive, affirming parental attitudes toward the children.

4. Clearly articulated expectations of moral conduct for the children.

5. Emotional security for each child, expressed verbally with frequency.

6. A stable spiritual environment, free of hypocrisy.

7. Appropriate, openly expressed affection between Mom and Dad.

8. No two-bedroom homes with Dad sleeping on the couch or the basement hideaway.

9. Openness to hearing contrarian thinking from children, without critical judgment.

10. Standards of conduct clearly spelled out.

Know any Christian families like this? Probably not. Even your own. We're setting the bar high, as well we should. Scripture has high expectations of believers. "You shall be perfect, just as your father in heaven is perfect" (Matthew 5:48). Now, that's a standard of exceptionally high expectation. Impossible? This isn't a book of theological exegesis meant to parse exactly what's meant by "perfect." But I can tell you this, most Christian families aren't even coming close to being "average," let alone faultless.

And this Top Ten list of what makes a family good isn't exhaustive. We actually wanted a Top Forty, but felt that might seem a little pretentious, let alone attainable. So, reader, consider your family fortunate that we aren't going to ask more of you. (Relax, that's for our next book.)

INSANITY AND THE OUIJA BOARD

Morris and Tina thought they had a "good" Christian family. They went to church regularly. They even read the Bible around the tree at Christmastime. Morris worked hard on two jobs, and Tina was busy looking after a new toddler. That left a lot of time on the hands of Adam, their older son, who had little supervision. He hadn't been a bad kid, but in the past year things had gotten out of hand. According to him, it all started with "the voices." Curse words. Salacious thoughts. Even blasphemy. At first he told no one. But as his life disintegrated, he finally opened up.

Like most Christians in America, his parents never considered the possibility that this might be demonic. When he started spitting out obscure names that sounded satanic, his parents rushed him to the ER room at the local hospital. From there, it was straight to the psych ward. He was diagnosed with anxiety disorder with borderline paranoid schizophrenia. A potpourri of pills was prescribed, but Adam quit them because he hated the foggy-brain side effects. A psychologist listened to

Adam's thoughts of suicidal ideation and concluded that the diagnosis was bipolar disorder.

Someone at church suggested that they have a pleasant Pentecostal pastor bless the house, so they did. Unfortunately, it didn't help much. After that, the voices were joined by the appearance of shadows following Adam and strange, creaking sounds in his bedroom. So much for throwing around a little anointing oil. The hospital psychiatrist wanted to up the medication. Still, Adam refused. He told his parents, "I'm not crazy. The voices are real. The sounds and shadows aren't my imagination."

Mom and Dad had no idea what to do by that point. They eventually swallowed their Baptist pride and took Adam to a priest. The clergyman freaked out when he heard the story and insisted that they go the medical route. Even if he thought Adam needed an exorcism, it might take six months to a year to get approval. And there was no guarantee that reciting some prayers from an ancient book would work even if the family was willing to wait.

Someone suggested, "Maybe your house is haunted." So, they checked out the history of the house. Sure enough, it was built on ancient Indian burial grounds said to be the dwelling place of ancestral spirits. A charismatic friend told them to "prayer walk" around the house, so they did. Adam got a little better. But the voices and the shadows came back. That's when Adam found our ministry on the Internet. He had stumbled onto our YouTube Exorcism Channel and saw a few of the hundreds of recorded-live exorcisms featuring real cases of demonic possession. Adam called our offices and convinced his parents to drive four hours for a Personal One-on-One Encounter session.

To listen to all the family tales of fear and trembling about what was going on with Adam, it certainly sounded like he was under some kind of demonic attack. But why? Wasn't this a "good" Christian family? Maybe. Maybe not.

A few probing questions revealed a lot of skeletons in the family closet. Dad, it turned out, had a bit of temper problem. And occasionally he drank too much. Mom appeared to be a bit of an enabler with Dad's issues. That probably was due to the fact that she was on her third marriage and didn't want this one to crash. More information came out as we examined the family dynamics more deeply. Adam reported that he had seen little affection at home, either toward him or between his parents. Not that this was what totally caused Adam's slide into mental instability. But it left him feeling emotionally unstable and in need of something to give clear direction in life.

That's why Adam was glad to find the Ouija board. This revelation came when he was asked point-blank what he thought was the negative turning point in his life. His parents reacted with shock and disbelief.

"I was in the garage one day, tinkering around," Adam explained. "I was bored and started rummaging through a pile of boxes that had been stored there forever. It was thrown in with some old tools and stuff. I pulled it out and decided to try it."

Adam's eyes began blinking erratically, and he became decidedly nervous. "All I knew about the Ouija board was what I'd seen in the movies, you know like *The Exorcist*. So, I started asking some questions. It spelled out a name. Azel. I'd never heard that word before. It sounded strange and got me more curious. One question and answer led to another. Soon I was having a long conversation with whatever was answering me through the board. Then the voices started. Not just Azel but others too. Even more strange names. Soon the voices were with me all the time, day and night. I couldn't get away from them. But what really got scary was when they told me to kill myself. Not just once, but over and over. 'KILL, KILL, KILL' they said, screaming in my head. I couldn't take it anymore and life started to become unreal."

Until then, Adam had been somewhat in control of his emotions. Not now. He began weeping, which quickly turned into hysterical wails.

"Make them go way," he cried out, over and over. "I burned the board. I don't even have it anymore. It's gone but the voices won't leave."

I (Bob) leaned over and put an arm around Adam to emotionally stabilize him. His parents did nothing. They just sat there. Perhaps they were too much in shock to respond. Maybe their aloofness was just more of what Adam had seen at home on a daily basis: two parents disengaged and clueless.

We don't want to be too hard on them. They both came from damaged backgrounds, but let's not too easily let them off the hook either. A Christian home with an Ouija board stored in the garage? How irresponsible is that? Even if they weren't well-versed regarding the dangers of such a demonic device, it's common knowledge, especially in evangelical Christian circles, that the Ouija board is a lot more than a game. They were thoughtless at best, willfully negligent at worst.

Thankfully this story ended on a positive note. More on that in a moment. But let's stop to consider what really makes a good or bad family.

WHAT MAKES A GOOD FAMILY?

"Good" and "bad" are relative—and extreme—words to use. Both words are hard to quantify, but to be practical, let's assume that they lie at opposite ends of the spectrum of what a Christian home ought to look like. Let's keep these words in mind as we discuss the criteria established above for what makes a family strong, functional, spiritual, and successful.

Strong bonds of communication between husband and wife. Communicating clearly with those nearest to us is one of the most difficult tasks to which God has called us. Our very existence as Christians depends upon relationships. First to God, to love him with all our hearts and minds. Then to our neighbors, to love them as we love ourselves. Finally, to those nearest to us in our families. Face it, it's often easier to love those at some distance than those within the family. Closeness brings friction, emotional territorial barriers, and competitiveness.

Often just getting along with a spouse or siblings is hard enough, but forging strong bonds is even more difficult.

Communication in a good family starts at the top with parents who talk regularly and effectively with each other. A bad family is characterized by spotty conversations, generally without much depth. Homes with troubled children are characterized by moms and dads who seldom have much to say to each other, beyond the basic "hellos," "goodbyes," and "what's for dinner." And parents who don't do well talking to each other generally do an even worse job of verbally and emotionally connecting to their children. Surely, one of Adam's parents knew about the Ouija board in that box. Perhaps over the course of time it might have come up in conversation and been disposed of. Lack of close communication was not the only problem leading to Adam's plight, but it didn't help either.

We'll talk later in the book about how to have good conversation in the home. For now, we need to establish that healthy dialogue between siblings, parents, and parent to child will only occur when it's nurtured and valued. That means everyone turning their cell phones off at dinner; restricting the television to viewing at appointed times instead of leaving it on as background noise, and finding mutually interesting things to banter about on a regular basis. Enough of parents and children living in their own private worlds. Children shouldn't have to compete with Dad for gaming time on the computer. Mom shouldn't be so busy with her coffee klatch that she's hardly ever around. Good communication means actually spending time as a family unit. Talk to your kids now, or you may be talking to them someday under far less pleasant circumstances, like Morris and Tina.

Emotional, spiritual, and sexual intimacy in the marriage. Yes, there will be a sex section in this book. This isn't it. Here we want to address the idea of intimacy on all levels as normative in a good home. It isn't that bad homes have no intimacy; it's just that it's sporadic and superficial. In too many homes parents say little to their children, and when they do talk it's not about anything significant in the child's life.

Good families talk about real-life things their kids are facing. Conversations go beyond "How are you?" "Fine."

If you can have the same conversation with a neighbor's kid that you have with your own child, that's not parent–child intimacy. If the only time you pray with them is at meals, your communication is not spiritual. If you've never listened to your child share a doubt or fear in honesty, you are likely not emotionally connected to your offspring. Consider the interaction with Adam's parents in the story above. Adam was talking to a counselor, a stranger, about profoundly damaging family secrets. And this was after the family had already made the rounds of doctors and psychiatrists! Why hadn't Tina and Morris gotten the truth out of Adam before? There was an obvious lack of familial connection in the home.

Positive, affirming parental attitudes toward the children. It seems apparent to say that good parents say good things to their kids, and bad parents say bad things. But what's good and bad? Certainly, esteem-building comments are good, and profane epithets are bad. But what are some other guidelines?

Many psychologists today admit that several generations of overdosing kids on "positive self-esteem" has created a generation of narcissistic youth with an outsized sense of entitlement. We've so indulgently affirmed them that they've become spoiled by an overabundance of praise. That's good, gone bad. But I would insist that such cases are not the norm. What we see more of is that most families fail to encourage their children enough.

Children tell us, "Dad is never happy when my grades are good, only mad when they're bad," or "It seems like my accomplishments don't get noticed, but my failures do." Too many parents don't know how to change "faint praise" into authentic reinforcement. Later in the book, we'll offer some suggestions. But for now, just know that good parents find genuine things to compliment and they avoid making demeaning or dismissive statements to their children.

Clearly articulated expectations of moral conduct for the children. Bad parents leave their children wondering how to behave; good parents set reasonable moral goals and assist in attaining them. The so-called "moral purity" movement has both its upside and downside (and plenty of critics), but we feel that the idea of calling your children to a holy life as they approach puberty is laudable. We've done that with all three of our daughters and we will describe how later in the book. Each of them has been taught the facts of life from an anatomic, emotional, and spiritual perspective, with a Christian overview.

More than that, we've tried to guide them through the labyrinth of ideas in the evangelical marketplace about how to interact with the opposite sex. We are bothered by constructs of morality based on legalism and culturally unreasonable modes of behavior that lead to Christian asceticism. Beyond the date–don't-date debate and the kiss-before-marriage-or-not argument, there are some basic guidelines that families need to make plain. These are biblical expectations that set forth standards that are both reasonable and attainable. Virginity before marriage, no abortion, no drugs, no pornography, no yoga, nothing of the occult, no alcohol in the home—these are good places to start. In our family, body piercings and tattoos also make the list for both spiritual and practical reasons. Don't like our list? What's on your list? There's no virtue in silence or letting a thirteen-year-old decide on her own if she's going to come home with a ring in her belly button.

Perhaps most important, leave nothing to the imagination of a child. Lay it all out. They're entitled to disagree, and most will to some degree, at least in the teen years. Just be certain that your expectations are solidly grounded, both intellectually and spiritually. At times, Mom and Dad may be wrong; but what's important is that the children know that their parents do have some boundaries.

Emotional security for each child, expressed verbally with frequency. We already touched on this briefly above, but this aspect of parenting is so crucial and neglected that it deserves more attention. The majority of kids on drugs, men and women in prison, and youth involved in the occult seldom or never heard "I love you" in their homes. When we ask troubled people if they were loved by their parents, the answer is almost always affirmative. But often we find out that conclusion is presumptive when we move on to the next question: "Did your parents actually say they loved you? Did they verbalize it?" Response: "Yes. Well, I think so; I'm sure they must have said it." Or even more sadly, "Well, they never *actually* said it, but I'm sure they did love me."

In the home, there is no substitute for frequent "I love you's," and lots of hugs and kisses. It's so simple.

Some children are needier than others. Their emotional bank needs frequent deposits. In that case, say it more often. Speak. Say it. Show them that you mean it. Often! It's not just what you say but how often, and how sincerely, you say it.

One of the best ways to communicate security to your children is to pray regularly with them. In a bad home, prayers are formalities, if uttered at all. In a good home, prayer is an organic, natural part of the flow of life. Too many Christian parents who tuck their small children in bed with, "Now I lay me down to sleep..." give the impression that prayer is only a ritual for infants. As their children get older, the prayers became less frequent, until they don't happen at all. We're talking about evangelical homes here. Countless times a wayward youth has told us, "I can't remember the last time we prayed together as a family."

A stable spiritual environment, free of hypocrisy. To continue the point: A good family provides regular spiritual nurturing. A bad family minimizes or neglects regular spiritual exercises such as prayer and church attendance. Worse, family spiritual life may be a sham, a pretense of evangelical piety with no soul.

An astonishing number of evangelical youth report that they never or seldom see their parents pray outside of church. This might seem innocuous, but it's not. In fact, when families are not places of genuine spiritual nurture, all hell breaks loose—quite literally. Satan targets the spiritual vitality of families because he knows that if he can destroy that, not only will the individual family members be weakened, but so will the social and political structure around them. Good government, good families. Good churches, good families. The foundation for every culture is the family. It is the indispensable building block of neighborhoods, cities, and nations.

Wherever there are good families—two-parent, God-fearing, church-going families—there are usually safe and orderly neighborhoods. Where there are broken, predominantly single-parent, alcoholic-dominant families, there is crime, violence, and gang warfare. We understand that many parents in broken homes are trying to do their best, and that single moms have a difficult situation. Socioeconomic factors also play a role. But let's not avoid the inconvenient truth that a home where the father has abandoned his responsibilities will likely be a household in crisis. A home with two adults cohabiting without the permanency of marriage sends the wrong signal to a child, whose need for stability and a sense of belonging may make him resort to a gang.

Appropriate, openly expressed affection between Mom and Dad. Let's explore further the importance of heartfelt affection in the home. Kids see sex and eroticism everywhere—on TV, advertising, music videos, movies. It's virtually unavoidable in our world. What is normal? The only way they can know is to see spontaneous love and considerate affection displayed between their parents at home. In counseling, we find that kids notice when there's no real emotional warmth between Mom and Dad. (Sometimes the children must wonder subconsciously how there was ever enough physical attraction between their parents to get them conceived!)

Some kids tell us that they've *never* seen their parents kiss or hug. (Although often they point out that they have seen them argue a lot.) Naturally, the parents are probably replicating their own home life growing up.

The fact is that good families are warmly affectionate, while bad families are emotionally cold and distant. Don't excuse it, saying, "We're just not that kind of family," or "We show our emotions in other ways." Hogwash! You need help. Get some professional counseling. Take our

"Seven Steps to a Happy Marriage" Intervention Encounter. Read other solid Christian books on this subject; you'll find a whole shelf of them at your local Christian bookstore or online.

No two-bedroom homes with Dad sleeping on the couch or the basement hideaway. OK, we're not in the sex section yet, but we have to take a swipe at the glaring sexual dysfunction in far too many Christian homes. In good families, the parents have good sex; in bad families, they have bad sex, or almost none at all. And the parents actually think that the kids don't notice.

Even the best Christian parents have differences. Spats. Disagreements. Arguments. Even fights. Frankly, I've always been suspicious of couples who say they never argue. I want to ask them, "Do you have a pulse?" Even in good homes there is tension. Life is like that. Financial burdens can sometimes overwhelm. Sickness may produce stress. In-laws may intrude. Job pressures may interfere. All these pressures can sometimes make the best relationship a bit edgy. That's normal. But what's not right is when it goes on and on, and without intervention from a pastor, counselor, or mature Christian.

Prolonged difficulty can lead to emotional and sexual disengagement. Protracted distance between husband and wife (months, even years) changes a good family into a bad family. If you want your kids to be divorce-prone or to struggle in their own marriages, do nothing. Keep your separate sleeping arrangements. After all, it's not about the nocturnal location of your bodies but the paucity of soul-connection that opens a door of Satan to attack your home. If your marriage is troubled, we're not suggesting you jump back in bed to find healing in sex. You first need to get wise counsel and then good advice on reconnecting. But making sexual disconnectedness a permanent part of the family identity will place your marriage in bondage, and it will increase the risk that your children will do the same someday.

Openness to hearing contrarian thinking from children, without critical judgment. "My parents don't listen to me." Every parent goes through it, that stage of life when Mom and Dad don't understand.

Even the biblical patriarchs struggled with it; they just didn't mention it because they had other things to talk about.

Here is a mistake that bad families make. They think that listening equates with agreeing. So they refuse to hear the other side of the story and become autocratic, demanding. All parents know how strange the logic of a child or teenager can seem to an adult mind. It's hard to sit back and keep quiet as they spew unreasonable ideas.

As a parent, don't forget the crazy ideas you once had that made so much sense back then, even though it might be downright painful to your ego to listen, all the while thinking, "Has my child not listened to anything that I said?" Remember, this too shall pass. But a sure way to reinforce the bad behavior your child wants to espouse is to summarily shut them down—which may leave a lasting wound of rejection. Relax and let them express how they see the world, with all the intensity and passion of the misguided mind of a youth. This is important even when it comes to deeply held family convictions about spiritual matters. "All the other kids are going to that movie," "My best Christian friends listen to that kind of music." "It's not that late to stay out." "I hear that word all the time at my Christian school."

Your child may even challenge some of your deepest biblical convictions. It is discomforting, after all those years of Sunday school, to hear them question the Trinity or why a loving God would send anyone to an eternal Hell. This is when you need to be ready to give an answer (see 1 Peter 3:15), a reasonable reason for the faith you want them to have. And if you have a bad family which hasn't been communicating belief and doctrine all along the way, you may be in for a battle. Worse yet, you may need deliverance in your home. But that topic will also come later in the book.

Standards of conduct clearly spelled out. We talked earlier in this chapter about "expectations of conduct" but here we want to discuss the whole spectrum of how a good family knows what it believes and why. Every family operates a little differently. Variables include standards of cleanliness, the assigning of household chores, access to money, the amount of allowable time for electronic entertainment, and more. Some parents allow their kids to have a TV. Others (ours included) don't, insisting that TV time is a family event whenever possible. Some say no smartphones until age sixteen or later. Some consider it a matter of safety and convenience much earlier in life. Different strokes.

But in bad families nobody states the rules, and implicitly understood rules almost always get broken.

A good way to have a good family, and to set your family free, is to make sure everyone knows the guidelines. No elbows on the table at dinner? Good etiquette. No social media before homework? Good idea. Home by whatever? Nail it down. Bad families hang loose. Nobody knows what's acceptable and not. That leads to conflict, especially when Mom or Dad cracks down on something nobody knew was wrong. This can create resentment, which may be a huge open door for Satan. To keep your family free and the devil from your door, one healthy option is to have periodic family discussions when each child is reminded of what's expected of him or her.

ADAM'S HAPPY ENDING

There was a happy ending to Adam's story, at least in the short term. He renounced his involvement with the Ouija board and a successful deliverance followed. Adam learned his lesson and renewed his faith in Christ. He left our session a completely changed person, thinking in his right mind for the first time in many months. The demon of insanity that entered with Azel had been expelled, and with it the mental confusion that had disrupted Adam's life.

But had Morris and Tina learned their lesson? Time will bear that out. The most important spiritual part of this story isn't the dramatic exorcism that took place, but that Adam's parents recognized that their family was in need of much reorientation. Going forward they needed to ask tough questions of themselves, many of the same questions we posed in this chapter. Getting the answers right would determine whether or not their family, which had just been set free, would stay free.

Chapter Four

SECRETS, SHAME, AND SHACKLES

"What I'm about to tell you, I've never told anyone before!"

Laura and I have heard that said many hundreds of times during our Personal Encounter sessions. Sometimes it's the opening salvo that kicks off the start of ministry. Sometimes, it's in the middle. Unfortunately, it's often at the end when our appointment schedule doesn't allow us an ample opportunity to bring adequate resolution. Sometimes, even I am shocked by who says this, and what they say.

I hear this from teens and preteens. I hear it from millennials. I even hear it from senior citizens, some in their eighties and nineties. How can something so powerfully life-influencing be buried so deeply and for so long? How has an individual managed to keep silent when everything inside is crying out for understanding and resolution? What internal emotional mechanisms keep the lid so tight?

One such instance was an eighty-nine-year-old Christian grandmother. When her children approached me about scheduling an Encounter, I was hesitant. What could I possibly contribute to the lifelong faith of a nearly nonagenarian? When everyone had left the room except for a trusted prayer assistant, she leaned forward in her wheelchair and said, "There's something I have to tell you before I die."

What dark secret could possibly have been lurking in the faint, mental recesses of her mind? I wasn't sure that I wanted to know.

"When I was four years of age, I was molested. I've never told anyone before!"

Those in ministries of healing and deliverance hear similar confessions often. But from someone nearly ninety? Not so much. How could she have hidden such profound shame for more than eight decades? What mechanism of the psyche had kept her silent, shackled her to shame, and unable to utter those words "I've never..."

Before we explore that psychological phenomenon, let me tell what happened next. That too was unexpected.

I've often, in print and in person, made the statement that the molestation of a child almost always leads to demonization. My book *Jezebel: Defeating Your #1 Spiritual Enemy,* explains in much detail the spiritual dynamics at work in such situations. But was it possible that this dear, very elderly saint of God had...demons? There was only one way to find out.

As an exorcist, it's not a stretch to take Bible and cross in hand to stare down the clandestine demons that are hiding in the soul of someone who has spent years experimenting with the occult. It's almost a certainty that an individual with a lifetime of drug addiction or sexual dysfunction, stemming from an unhappy or abusive childhood, will have picked up severe spiritual oppression along the way. My books *Dealing with Demons* and *Curse Breaking* explain thoroughly the whys and wherefores of this cycle of demonic infestation. But the family members of this frail, wheelchair-bound woman testified that she had served the Lord all her life and had been active in lay ministry.

Yet, when I commanded any evil spirits that were tormenting her to come forth, she nearly sprang from her wheelchair. With her weak arms, she lifted herself to the fullest extent possible, and with a harsh, determined voice shouted, "What do you want with me. I've possessed her since she was a child, and I'm not leaving now."

Before me was an infirm woman, tethered to an oxygen tank, in a state of full-blown, demonic manifestation. A demon, Jezebel it turns out, was defiantly challenging my authority as a Christian and an exorcist. After about ten minutes of back and forth, me commanding and the demon resisting, the evil spirit that had entered her through sexual abuse eighty-five years earlier was expelled. After a brief struggle following my declaration, "Go to the Pit," she fell back in her chair, exhausted and just as shocked as I was. A smile filled her face, an expression she hadn't been able to muster for a very long time. She was free. Not long after, she passed away. And she was able to live her last few months free of the evil spirit that had harassed her for so long.

There is much to be gleaned from this incident, but my main purpose in telling this story is to underscore these salient points:

- There is no limit, short of death, to the time when any individual can receive healing and deliverance.

- Demonic forces are capable of concealing their presence for long periods of time, even in the most spiritually astute hosts in which they have embedded their evil.

- The pernicious power of shame and secrecy can reduce even the strongest person, spiritually speaking, to a vessel bound by the tragedies of the past.

FAMILY SECRETS

Your family, my family, every family—has secrets. Some are relatively harmless, spiritually innocuous. They contain no moral or spiritual toxicity. These tidbits about family foibles are the subject of family-gathering conversations, often producing laughter or wryly raised eyebrows. But the secrets that keep families from being free are the source of relational poison and demonic attachments. The uncle that everyone knows "likes" little girls. The mysterious aunt who foretold the sex of babies with a weighted string. The distant grandfather, several generations back, whom it was rumored killed a man over a woman. The cousin who went to prison for dealing drugs. The sweet grandmother who cheated and had at least one child who didn't look like grandpa.

These cases of family turpitude may be whispered away as family canards and left unspoken until the next family reunion when everyone gets together and something raises the issue again. But to the victim of real evil, such as incest, molestation, violent discipline, rampant promiscuity, or illegal actions, it's no joke. Just one such injustice might have been the source of many years of emotional anguish and demonic misery.

What to do? There is a right and a wrong way to expose family secrets, which we will discuss below. But truly egregious behavior must not be left unexposed or dismissed without accountability. To truly set your family free you must be willing to open every door to darkness in the family bloodline. Every family has secrets, and some should be kept in the family. But other transgressions must be held morally, spiritually, and sometimes legally accountable.

Why tell? Some acts are illegal! Why are some secrets worthy of exposure to the light of moral condemnation? First, some are illegal, such as the sexual abuse of a minor by an adult. Authorities may need to be notified. Many times Laura and I have been responsible for giving sound advice to victims of abuse, and that advice has led to the arrest and conviction of individuals who broke the law. Incest of a minor child is a crime. The forced sexual submission of a family member is a crime. I've known of instances where a brother-in-law, for example, raped a sister-in-law and that man's own wife didn't want him reported to the law and prosecuted. I've had to confront a wife who knew that her husband was sexually abusing one of their children. She said nothing for fear of losing the husband and father who was the sole financial support of the family. As an accomplice to the crime, she said nothing lest the family be ripped apart and impoverished. So-called "harsh discipline," where actual injury to the body of child occurs, is also a legally punishable offense. Any family member who knows it is going on has a duty to report it to Child Protective Services.

Why tell? Some acts are emotionally damaging! If a parent is verbally abusing a child or a spouse is verbally abusing their partner to the extent that mental impairment may result, there needs to be intervention. This matter is a bit subjective, and a lot depends on the motive and the measure of the abuse. But the things Laura and I have had people relate to us regarding their emotional abuse from a family member are genuinely outrageous. For example, we've had people tell us:

1. A parent calling a female child a slut or whore.

2. An extended family member threatening physical harm, even to the point of saying that the victim will be killed if they blab.

3. A mother or father saying that they wish they had aborted their child.

4. A child making life-threatening statements to a parent, saying, for instance, "I will kill you if you don't do this!"

5. A parent participating in sexually outrageous behavior in front of a child. I've had people tell me that when they were a kid they were allowed to witness their parents having sex. Some even say that they were invited to join their naked parents in a hot tub or spa. Some children were around when their "swinging" parents had a threesome.

6. I've had children tell me that their parents didn't shield them from drug-taking behavior or fall-down-drunk

episodes, even offering alcohol and recreational drugs to the offspring.

Why tell? Some acts are demonic door-openers. If you know of a family member who takes a child to a psychic or has them participate in forms of witchcraft or shamanism, speak up. Don't be afraid to tell an in-law or extended family member that New Age practices can lead to demon possession. If you are aware that someone in the immediate or larger family uses an Ouija board or practices some form of divination, let your biblical convictions be known. Don't stay silent. You don't have to act like a super-Christian bringing the hammer down on their spiritually illicit actions. Be gracious and reasonable, but firm. Don't look the other way. The secret that you expose might be the iceberg's tip of much more appalling behavior that will be unveiled.

WHO NEEDS TO KNOW FAMILY SECRETS?

If something illegal or immoral has happened to you or a family member of your bloodline or extended family, to whom should you reveal the evil?

James 5:16 contains an important injunction that undergirds not only inner healing ministry but is an important counseling principle. Let's consider this passage in several translations:

> *Confess your faults one to another, and pray one for another, that ye may be healed.* (KJV)

> *Confess your trespasses to one another, and pray for one another that you may be healed.* (NKJV)

> *Therefore confess your sins to each other and pray for each other so that you may be healed.* (NIV)

Whichever translation the reader may prefer ("faults," "trespasses," or "sins"), the main intent of James' message is that the sharing of personal failures, especially disclosing deeply buried bondages, brings healing. It is "telling"—the sharing of these secrets to another (we shall shortly suggest to whom)—that brings remediation to the soul. We are "healed" when we entertain the process of confessional relationships. Exposing the secrets of the soul to the right person in the right situation is one method of soul-cleansing. All this was revealed nineteen hundred years before Freud and his followers developed the psychoanalytical model of counseling.

But for your family to be free from the shameful secrets of the past, you must carefully consider to whom you bare you soul, how much you tell them, and the circumstances under which this purging occurs. First some advice. A friend, even a trusted Christian friend, isn't always the best person for several reasons. Friendships can turn sour over time. Do you really want someone who has betrayed your trust to know the intimate details of your life? Laura and I both have Christian friends with whom we've shared deeply personal matters, but these are individuals with whom we've walked in fellowship for *decades*, not just a few years. These confidants have proven their walk with Christ, and trustworthiness, through many shared struggles. They are truly a friend who, as Proverbs 18:24 says, "sticks closer than a brother."

Even a pastor may not qualify as an intimate person capable of hearing private matters of the heart and responding maturely. At the least, be certain that the pastor from whom you seek counsel is someone you want to know your more private issues, when you behold his face week after week in the pulpit and shake his hand as you leave church each Sunday.

Furthermore, many pastors are simply not professionally qualified to offer advice about matters of a severe psychological nature. Their seminary or Bible School education may not have prepared them to offer insights on things such as sexual abuse, self-injury, addictions, or the many mental health issues that may hold a family in bondage. Our International School of Exorcism has extensive courses on the various schools of psychological thought. Such knowledge can help guide someone who is seeking a licensed therapist. The School also has excellent material outlining the various mental health issues that a family may face, such as borderline personality disorder, schizophrenia, and bipolar disorder, to mention a few of the areas covered.

What matters most about seeking professional counseling? In many ways, if it's accessible where you live and not unreasonably expensive, such intervention is a better option than local ministerial advice. But be careful. The counselor you seek may have no regard for Christian principles, or worse yet be steeped in New Age ideas. Even many Christian counselors won't accept the idea of demonic spiritual oppression, and definitely not the idea that a Christian can be demonized. Whatever help they give will end if the counseling process encounters the interference of evil spirits. And I must add a warning about seeking deliverance without due diligence beforehand. Be cautious about someone uttering prayers for freedom from demons. There are many fine deliverance ministries, but there are also very many which are not credible and do more harm than good. Carefully study the ministry you are considering before meeting with them. With whom are they affiliated? What is their theological model for healing and deliverance? Do they have printed materials, especially seriously written books, which lay out their strategy for healing prayers?

Permit me to use our ministry as an example. We have, at this point in time, thirty-six published books laying out in detail our beliefs, our doctrines, and our template for deliverance ministry. Several of the books (some five hundred pages or more) are used as textbooks in Bible colleges and seminaries. Our work has reached more than a hundred countries. I am a visiting professor at Bible colleges, training students in spiritual warfare. Our International School of Exorcism is a credible academic institution grounded in an understanding of both church history and the theology of deliverance ministry. Please understand, we're not patting ourselves on the back, but demonstrating some criteria by which you can evaluate the credibility of a ministry. We aren't saying that a ministry helping someone in need of spiritual warfare must necessarily have equal accolades before it is qualified. We're merely suggesting benchmarks by which any individual evaluates to whom they open up the deepest parts of their soul. Do your homework and be certain that the ministry from which you seek help is credible and effective. If nothing else, seek referrals of those who have received ministry from the group or individual offering this kind of help.

SHARING SECRETS WITH THE FAMILY

We've explored to whom you should or should not share secrets outside the family, but what about inside the family? Who needs to know what? What should spouses tell each other and how much disclosure is appropriate between parents and children?

Children should tell parents. So long as a child is underage, complete transparency is usually necessary. It's hard to think of a situation where a minor child would be justified in keeping a secret from a parent, if the parent is loving and emotionally healthy. The child who trusts peers and siblings with morally relevant information, while keeping the parent in the dark, is opening a door to spiritual oppression. If a child has tried drugs or experimented sexually, the parent needs to know. If a child has a friend, even one who professes to be a Christian, and that friend is involved in some kind of illegal or immoral activity, the parent should be informed.

There are situations where this measure of openness might be restricted. If one or both of the parents are mentally ill or emotionally impaired in any way, a different set of issues may be faced. A "Catch-22" situation may develop. For example, if a child has been sexually abused, and if telling the parent will result in shaming and even possible blaming of the victim, someone other than the parent may be a more reliable outlet. In this case a pastor or school counselor may be a better choice. Just be certain that when seeking help the person turned to possesses reasonable emotional health and has a strong internal, emotional structure. The family with a parent who is outside the boundaries of sound mind and conscience may need to retain professional help and even legal assistance.

Be careful what you tell your spouse. In a spiritually and emotionally healthy marriage, total openness may be possible. But some relationships may not be mature enough for one or both of the partners to know everything about their mate. That's where a professional counselor, a priestly confessional, or a therapeutic setting may be needed. Considering the couples that Laura and I have counseled, we've seen marriages both strengthened and damaged by confidential disclosures. Before you tell your spouse "everything," think for a moment if what you share will build greater intimacy or make the relationship more fragile. And consider how much you should share.

Take, for example, a marriage in which there has been infidelity. In most cases, the offended spouse needs to know about the affair. But limits should be set on the details that may be revealed. This is where an arbitrator, such as a licensed marriage counselor with experience in these matters, may negotiate the conversation. Holding back information may create further suspicion. Telling too much may result in information overload that the offended spouse has difficulty handling. What was intended to be a healing admission may instead irreparably wound the heart of the aggrieved spouse, who afterward may find it difficult to forgive. To be blunt, as a case in point, the unfaithful spouse should admit to the moral treachery, but it would not be wise to tell how many times they had sex during the adultery, or how much they enjoyed the sex. If there is no effective outside third party to intervene, any disclosures should be handled prayerfully and cautiously.

When it comes to disclosing past occult history to a spouse, generally the more information the better. In this way, there can be marital agreement in prayer to overcome any lingering demonic bondage. I do caution couples to be wary of trying to do deliverance on a spouse. I have known some couples who ministered to each other in this way successfully; but I know more cases in which this led to spiritual abuse and even threatened the marriage. When trying to cast demons out of your spouse, the evil spirits might spill the beans about more than you wanted to know. Or the demons may play upon challenges in the relationship to pit one against the other. When it comes to casting demons, in most cases, leave it to the "professionals."

Secrets That Shame

Some family secrets are healthy, if they pertain to issues that only a family may need to know: the insecurities of a child regarding his or her appearance; a parent's struggle with substance abuse that is being properly addressed by addiction counseling; areas of growth in faith and doubts about one's standing with God; the latest love interest of a teenage child; family spats concerning issues that are being prayed about and being addressed properly; even the possibility of a family member being demonized due to some sin that the general public need not be aware of.

But beware secrets that shame. To have proper boundaries regarding shame, consider briefly the differences between healthy and unhealthy shame.

Shame that leads to repentance. There is legitimate and illegitimate shame; honest and dishonest shame. Both result in feelings of disgrace or self-condemnation. Legitimate shame comes from authentically negative actions and the feelings resulting from some egregious behavior. True shame is the result of the conscience, the inner voice God has given to each soul, speaking back to us that what we've done has violated some legal or moral stricture. Shame can be a helpful guide to establishing limits on human behavior, whether it comes from social taboos or biblical edicts.

Jeremiah 8:12 speaks of the denial of real shame by alluding to those Hebrews who committed spiritual "abominations." The prophet rhetorically asks, "Were they ashamed when they had committed abomination? No! They were not at all ashamed. Nor did they know how to blush." This condemnation of spiritually heinous acts was doubly shameful. First, the people of God had the Law of Moses and knew right from wrong by divinely communicated edict. Second, as the apostle Paul points out in Romans 2:5, the moral law of god is written in the heart of every person, and that "their conscience also bears witness." This witness leads to the inner response of conscience, which, by the thoughts of man, internally accuses or excuses. Thus, real shame for real transgression should be accompanied by real repentance.

Shame that sears the soul. "He brought this on himself." Heard that? Or, "He should be ashamed of himself." These assessments might be true, but might also be shaming statements intended to falsely brand someone with unwarranted guilt. False shame sears the soul by name-calling or ridicule to destroy human dignity. Sometimes specious shame is used in relationships to get the best of another. In a bad marriage or parent–child relationship, this kind of shame is accusatory and often without substance.

Unhealthy self-shaming often follows a personal violation, such as rape, molestation, incest, and other sexual sins. It can also accompany physical abuse by a parent. In these cases, the victim is revictimized by heeding the self-induced voices that falsely assume fault for the immoral, even illegal, actions of others.

In counseling, Laura and I often witness this effect with those who were violated as children. The mind of a child quite naturally assumes that a parent is perfect, and if someone is at fault, it must be the child. Even in cases of incest, there is often shaming by the offending parent, who can't admit their own moral failure.

Shame projected by someone with a narcissistic personality disorder may make the shamed individual feel despicable. The person despised by the narcissist, such as a spouse, may react to the shaming with relational aggression. This shamed person may even try to retaliate with bullying or anger in response to the projected shame. Thus, the illegitimate shaming causes both the narcissist who shames, and also his/her victim to engage in an increasing cycle of mutual abuse.

BREAKING THE SHACKLES OF SHAME

The shackles of shame can be broken if the falsely shamed person follows the steps outlined in this chapter:

1. Understand that every family has secrets, but healthy families place boundaries on harboring concealed falsehoods.

2. Wisdom is needed to determine which concealments are inappropriate, damaging, or even illegal.

3. Sharing secrets with family members should be approached cautiously, depending on the hierarchy of the relationship, that is, spouse to spouse or parent to child.

4. Healthy families know the difference between good and bad shame. Parents in emotionally and spiritually stable families will determine by much prayer and soul-searching when a child is to be shamed versus when such shaming is unwarranted and damaging to character development.

5. A good family will know when to seek help beyond the family structure to receive objective, spiritually sound advice on how to address delicate issues of improper concealment of information.

Chapter Five

CHRISTIANS DO THE DUMBEST THINGS

I admit it. The chapter title is a bit insulting. If Laura were titling this chapter I'm sure it would have been more diplomatic. She's more relationally skilled than me. I've always been a bit blunt and to the point. But I don't know a nice way to say this. One might think that a follower of Christ would be wiser and more discerning than the average atheist. Overall, that is probably true, because Christians, according to the Bible, possess the "spirit of truth" (John 16:13).

But not all Christians necessarily walk in the truth, wise counsel, and spiritual insight given by the Bible. Sometimes they do really, dumb things. Especially when it comes to the family. To illustrate, I've taken a few cases from my files. Don't gasp. These are actual, real-life situations Laura and I have encountered when counseling couples. Nonsignificant changes have been made to protect the identity of these individuals.

HAROLD AND KAREN—A STUDY IN MARITAL ABSURDITY

Karen and Harold had a troubled marriage by anyone's standards, even from a nonreligious perspective. Karen, a childhood victim of sexual abuse, had an affair about three years into the marriage. Harold found out, forgave, and tried to move on. The fact that they had three children was a mitigating factor causing him to stay in the relationship. Eventually, he too had an affair. Perhaps he was covertly getting even. Maybe he was tired of what had become a stale relationship over time.

But here's the twist. Harold maintained the semblance of a continuing marital relationship. He and Karen, and the whole family, took vacations together. They attended church together, except when business took him out of town for extended periods of two weeks to a month at a time. In fact, professional demands only required a few days out of those long periods of absence. The rest of the time? He was living with another woman across town.

It was a big city and Harold made sure that he and his "partner" didn't frequent any public places where his cover might be blown. This went on for years, and when Karen found out she then declared that she was OK with the set-up. Harold kept sending enough money to pay the mortgage and provide shelter when he was gone. When he was "home," he and Karen even engaged in periodic sexual relations. All this, of course, to keep the frayed edges of their absurdly bizarre cohabitation in place, at least until the kids were grown.

CLINT AND SONIA—LOST LOVE AND RELATIONAL INERTIA

Sonia didn't love her husband. The flame had gone out long ago. The marriage had morphed into a carefully, but unconsciously, negotiated business arrangement. Sonia had her own business as a Human Resources consultant, and Clint was employed by a marketing firm for a retail giant. "My youngest son is 14," Sonia said, to open the Encounter session. "He's a freshman. I've got four years to go, and then I can walk out," she explained.

Sonia also declared, with brokenness in her voice, "I don't know what else to do. Clint won't see a marriage counselor. My kids are the only thing that keep me going emotionally. And my work. It's very demanding, and in a way, that's good. There's no time to think about how I feel. If I stopped to think about how abandoned I am as a wife I'd probably have an emotional breakdown."

Sonia felt trapped by theology, which she felt wouldn't allow her to separate or contemplate divorce. She also didn't want to think about the stress of splitting up. It was easier to bury her personal needs under a pile of motherly duties and workplace demands. But after a few verbal exchanges with us, she admitted that she had caught her youngest child with marijuana and that her oldest daughter, who was seventeen, had gotten involved with an unsavory character who was obsessed with the occult.

Most of the advice Sonia got about her situation was bad. Her pastor said that she had no choice but to stay in the marriage. Her parents, who were themselves divorced, told her to put up with things, that starting over would be a lot more painful. Christian friends advised her to hang in there and keep praying and hoping for a miracle. Meanwhile, there was a certain man at work who was showing her a lot of attention. She feared she was falling for him.

ADRIAN AND SHERRY—MAKE-BELIEVE MARRIAGE AND A DANGEROUS LIAISON

Adrian was beside himself. He had no idea when he married Sherry what he was getting into. It was only after a few months beyond the honeymoon that she opened up about her chaotic upbringing. Though her parents maintained middle-class, suburban all-is-OK appearances, inside the four walls of home, life was a nightmare. Dad drank and mom cheated. Sherry once watched her dad beat her brother while he screamed for mercy because of a bone that had been broken by the "harsh discipline," as her dad called it. Mom was so terrified that she eventually got a gun and once pointed it directly at dad threatening to pull the trigger. A sister was pregnant by age sixteen and was quickly rushed off to a local abortionist. Oh yeah, Sherry's parents were self-proclaimed "Holy-Ghost-filled, tongues-speaking Christians."

Adrian's sheltered, conservative evangelical life hadn't prepared him to be married to someone with so much baggage. So, he slipped into denial and went through the motions of marriage—engaging in irregular marital sex, smiling through annual family vacations, and medicating his pain with leftover pills from a minor surgical procedure. He spent more and more of his time at church, busy with a men's group, a Bible study, and regular services.

Meanwhile, Sherry plunged deeper and deeper toward clinical depression. Her personal appearance was less and less well-managed and she seldom ventured out of the house. Their three children seemed to be at each other's throats much of the time, and the most peaceful place Adrian could find was time spent with buddies from work, most of whom weren't Christians. They swore, drank, and occasioned "gentlemen's clubs" now and then. Adrian wondered how much longer he would hold out from joining their sinful lifestyle.

TEN LESSONS TO BE LEARNED FROM UNHAPPY HOMES

It goes without saying that the people I've described lived very miserable lives. These marriages were sources of emotional pain and dead-end hopes for the future. But each of them had several faults in common, as do a long list of similar accounts I could cite. And yes, each of these couples had severe degrees of demonization, requiring inner healing and deliverance. Here's a short list of a few things that these couples, and similar marriages, have in common:

1. Many faulty marriages exhibit a lack of due diligence during the dating and get-acquainted process. I've

found it ironic that people, especially those of spiritual faith, are more particular about the process of buying a house or a car than they are about selecting a mate who is capable of a healthy, emotionally, and spiritually equitable relationship.

2. When troubles and conflicts arise, as they will in any marriage, a rosy-colored naïveté sets in, a mindset that God is going to somehow work it all out if they just hang in there a little longer.

3. Bad marriages often survive on life support with the presumably noble idea that the estranged partners must stay together for the sake of the kids, no matter how miserable things get. We've already talked about this, but it deserves more attention here.

4. Couples in crisis tend to think that no one is really catching on to what's really happening. They convince themselves that the ruse of the relationship has everyone fooled, even their own children. They have lived the lie of their dysfunctional home so long that they think everyone else also buys into the mutual fantasy.

5. Couples in crises, especially Christians, have the idea that they can somehow fix things by themselves, given enough time. They determine that prayer and Christian fellowship alone will ameliorate their faults. They fail to see that objective intervention is necessary, and that without it they will never right the ship of the marriage by themselves. This too, we've discussed earlier, but will elaborate further here.

6. Christians in a rocky marriage seldom contemplate the possibility that either will have an affair until it's

too late. They forget that Satan is circling their weakened home and probably has someone already picked out as a potential tempter who will lead one or the other spouse astray. Jezebel never sleeps.

7. If one of the partners in a troubled marriage refuses to get counseling or healing intervention, the other person in the relationship can't go on forever, hoping against hope, and praying against all odds without a physical and emotional toll being taken. Sooner or later, something will break, and it might mean a mental health crisis.

8. Children in an out-of-sync home know what's happening. They may not be privy to all the ugly details, but they are aware that their parents are troubled, and wonder if they might be the reason. That conclusion is, of course, in error but the blame has to be put somewhere and the kids are often the ones who take the brunt of the finger-pointing.

9. Every troubled marriage has a tipping-point beyond which it might not be retrievable. Most couples in a damaged relationship usually don't take action soon enough. They wait until things are so bad that there may be nothing to salvage,

10. A sexless, loveless marriage isn't a marriage. It's an emotional corpse that one or the other partner drags around thinking that resuscitation is just around the corner.

If you think that I'm on a mission to tell you how I set straight the couples referenced above, that's not the point. What families need most in our confused and disjointed world is information on how to navigate the moral chaos and theological contradictions of our times.

Setting the family free from the bondage of past baggage and moral conundrums requires clear thinking and abandoning the shibboleths that prevent remedial action. If an individual is bound by old ways of thinking and widely held but faulty reasoning, there will be no clear path to real freedom.

Without wanting to appear insulting, I'm going to further explain what I think are the ten dumb things that married Christian couples do, based on the points above. I don't mean to imply that the people referenced previously are dumb. In all three examples, these individuals were bright, successful, and socially adept. It's what they did, what they believed about themselves, that was dumb.

TEN DUMB THINGS CHRISTIAN COUPLES BELIEVE

1. **Love conquers all.** Most dating couples follow a predictable romantic trajectory. They meet, hang out, develop attraction, begin dating, experience passion, fall in love, and start thinking about marriage. Often, they never meet each other's parents, or they've only met under the best of circumstances, like a holiday visit to his or her family. This is spiritually and relationally dangerous on many levels.

I prefer the old adage, "Fail to plan, plan to fail," and have used it descriptively many times in my writings because it says it all so simply. As applied to dating and marriage, it could be called the lack of "due-diligence dating/marriage."

As the reader likely knows, I'm a deliverance minister. It's my calling and spiritual specialty. One thing anyone quickly learns when they are involved in praying for those spiritually tormented is this: Most demonic bondage is generational; it is learned in the birth home and/or is inherited from the bloodlines of both parents. That's why it is critical to know as much as possible about the spiritual background of the person who is being considered as a potential mate.

If you discover that the love of your life has a lot of demonic baggage, it's not a deal-killer. But you don't want to go forward until those matters have been adequately addressed. That may involve considerable time spent with inner healing and possibly exorcism.

What questions should you ask of someone you're falling in love with? It's probably best to seek help from someone such as me, or a deliverance ministry we can recommend. But for starters you want to know these basic things about your beloved:

- Has anyone in the family been involved in witchcraft or New Age practices? If so, what specific forms of divination did they engage in? All such occult alliances need to be renounced and any curses broken which are related to these indulgences. Perhaps your romantic partner has received some deliverance. Find out how much and what it entailed. Not all those who claim to cast out demons are credible, and sometimes the cure is worse than the cause.

- What kinds of illegal or immoral activities have taken place in the extended family structure? To the uninformed, what I'm about to say may sound extreme, but I've known of many naïve men and women who've unknowingly married into a family where incest and sexual abuse is rife. Others find out after marriage that one or more family members is addicted to alcohol or drugs or has engaged in criminal activity. These issues can be resolved *if* you know in advance. But these are not skeletons you want protruding from a closet after you've embarked on marital bliss.

- Does your future marriage partner have any personal addictions to alcohol, drugs, or pornography? What steps at rehabilitation have been taken? How severe is the addiction? If you're uncomfortable asking these questions, that's a red flag by itself. At least be certain that a pastor or qualified spiritual counselor has asked those questions. And this is very important—

don't embark on marriage with the idea that love will conquer all and that the problems will go away once connubial pleasantries set in.

2. **I'm OK, you're OK.** I borrow this subsection title from the 1969 self-help book about transactional analysis by author Thomas Anthony Harris. The book was sometimes wrongly construed to be an imprimatur of mutually self-affirming behavior. In fact, this best-selling book (15 million copies) postulated Four Life Positions: I'm OK, You're OK; I'm OK, You're Not OK; I'm Not OK, You're OK; and I'm Not OK, You're Not OK. It's the latter classification I want to reference.

In marriage, it's more often "I'm Not OK, You're Not OK." If there is mutual fault leading to marriage misfiring, hanging in there isn't going to make it all better. In fact, it's more likely to get worse. Evangelical Christians are often guided by a misunderstanding of Bible verses such as 1 Corinthians 13:7 that encourage followers of Christ to "hope all things, endure all things" as an act of love. Clearly, some boundaries are needed. A wife can't be expected to "endure" life-threatening domestic violence, though some misguided pastors have given such bad advice. Having "hope" is good, but a marriage on the rocks in which verbally abusive behavior has become commonplace can't be salvaged with rosy expectations. There are some marital situations where time will hurt more than heal, and decisive action to save the marriage is necessary.

3. **It's better for the kids.** This fallacy of perpetuating marital misery for the family's sake has already been addressed in an earlier chapter, but let's focus here on priorities. Many couples that come to Laura and me for ministry are shocked when I point out that the husband–wife relationship takes precedence over the parent–child relationship. They've assumed, and have sometimes been told by well-meaning Christians, that the welfare of children is more important than any bumps along the marriage journey. That's decidedly incorrect.

Before there were children, God created Adam and Eve and sanctified their relationship as primary to the fulfilling of His purposes on earth. Husband and wife are "one flesh." It is to each other that they are to "cleave." I'm not dismissing the importance of parental responsibilities to children. Quite the contrary. It is through the healthy conjoining of a man and woman in marriage that children enjoy the best chances at success in life. Children are to take their cues to spiritual and emotional health from the parents, not vice versa. Healthy marriage, strong children. Unhealthy marriage, morally weak children.

4. No one knows what's behind closed doors. Few couples can hide their marital discord from the outside world. Even fewer can hide it from the children. They are living a lie that no one believes. A marriage in stress sends off powerfully negative signals that are hard to conceal. Friends and acquaintances sometimes see the impending marital shipwreck before either spouse is aware of what's really happening. The husband and wife may think that they have a vested interest in living a lie, but outsiders do not. Friends may cringe at harsh words spoken between couples while the married pair has become so used to slighting and insulting each other that they barely notice any more. A wife may endure put downs with a shrug of the shoulders, while her girlfriends are horrified that a man would speak to a woman that way.

Perhaps the dumbest thing that couples in a bad marriage believe is that the children don't notice the bitterness and ill will. When couples no longer express warm, natural affection the children are aware that the spark is gone. When the bedroom door is no longer locked, or mom and dad retreat each evening to separate quarters, the kids aren't clueless. They may not have all the intricacies of marital malfunction figured out, but they know that something is terribly wrong between their parents.

5. We don't need any help to make our marriage better. You may be an uber-Christian—singing in the choir, teaching Sunday school, attending every prayer meeting and seminar, watching Christian TV five hours a day, volunteering at the rescue mission, double tithing, and fasting once a week—and still not save your own deteriorating marriage. Marriage repair isn't a do-it-yourself skill. When couples tell me that they'll restore their own mangled marriage, I simply reply, "If you could have, you would have."

This matter we've also addressed before, but like so many points to be addressed in this book, you can't say it enough: Marriages repair from the outside in, not the inside out. There is no more powerful soul-connection on earth than marriage. It is the ultimate bond. The King James word "cleave" in Genesis 2:24 actually means "glued together." We even adopt that imagery in our language and culture. We speak of being "stuck on you" or "she's sure stuck on him." Ever notice how long-married couples start looking and acting like each other? They are so much "one flesh" (Genesis 2:24; 1 Corinthians 6:16) that many of their individual characteristic blend over time.

From a deliverance and spiritual warfare perspective, what one spouse has, the other one gets. That means that all the unsanctified spiritual garbage, all the unbroken curses, all the demons, and spiritual oppression of your spouse can land on you. As pointed out earlier, this is one reason to so carefully investigate the moral and spiritual background of your potential mate. And if you're already married, be aware that the spiritual weaknesses of your marriage partner may become, to some extent, part of your spiritual identity.

Consequently, if there are two people yoked together with similar marital detritus, how reasonable is it to assume that they can pull themselves up out of the same spiritual pit?

6. **Real Christians don't break their marriage vows**. This too is a topic previously addressed, but more needs to be said here: Assuming fidelity will endure in a failed marriage can be foolhardy. Only a narcissist, sociopath, or moral pervert would really want to have an affair. Certainly, a Christian man or woman, who started a marriage believing in "happily ever after," would never embark on a deliberate path to adultery. But a broken marriage risks entertaining open arms, and opportunities for unfaithfulness are all too readily available in our time of the Internet and social media. It's easy to find someone willing to

break up a home. Even I am shocked to hear stories from an unfaithful spouse about how casually they fell into the arms of another person.

There are no longer any scarlet letters in Hollywood. In fact, the entertainment media treats having an affair as the "normal" right of an unhappy spouse. Christians in North America have watched many prominent preachers run around on their wives, ditch them, and then almost immediately marry the woman with whom they were sexually involved. The result is a collective shell-shock, a kind of moral PTSD that afflicts evangelicals to the point that no amount of morally appalling behavior is noteworthy.

People have needs. Emotional needs to be wanted. Sexual needs to be physically fulfilled. Relational needs to have companionship. If all, or part of that, is missing in a marriage, eyes may lust and feet may stray. The spirit of Jezebel, the dominant demon of our age, is on the loose with mega-intensity. (Read my book *Jezebel: Defeating Your #1 Spiritual Enemy* if you have any doubts. Jezebel's M. O. is control, manipulation, witchcraft, and sexuality. And Jezebel has plenty of willing victims in today's erotically obsessed culture. And since, as I explain in my book, the spirit of Jezebel can possess either men or woman, neither spouse is safe when the home fires aren't burning as they used to.)

7. **I can stay in this bad marriage and not be damaged.** No you can't. A bad marriage takes a toll on both parties. Remaining in a destructive relationship without insisting on intervention may result in irreparable impairment. A lot can suffer. Health can suffer. The inner toxicity of stress may break down normal bodily functions. Mental health may be the first to go. Depression, delusion, even suicidal ideation may result. Spiritual deterioration is usually present. When your noncooperative spouse quits going to church, you may do the same. I've encountered countless bad marriages where the one spouse who tried to hang on to the Lord eventually gave up out of emotional exhaustion.

Bitterness, anger, unforgiveness, even revenge—all of these develop over time in an unresolved bad marriage. You can't pray enough to stop every negative consequence from occurring. I must repeat again. Laura and I don't want you to get a divorce and give up on the marriage, unless there is due cause such as rampant unfaithfulness or constantly escalating physical danger. But the suffering spouse, stuck in a marriage where their partner will do nothing to correct horrendous ills afflicting the relationship, must never forget this important fact: If you are a Christian, you are the temple of the Holy Spirit and you were purchased by the death of Jesus Christ on the cross (see 1 Corinthians 1:18–20). By not seeking constructive action to change the corrupt dynamics of your marriage, you are dishonoring your own self. That is a sin, and one that will open you to spiritual oppression.

If one of the family members, affected by the marriage crisis, refuses spiritual intervention, the party seeking help must not subordinate their concerns to the one preferring to remain silent and inert.

8. **I'm hanging on to this dying marriage so the kids don't suffer.** Or so you say. In reality, children are the first casualties in a toxic, poisoned marriage. We've already addressed this briefly above, and in previous parts of the book, but let's take another look at how this lie plays out. Almost every time I talk with families in crisis, the parents tell me that the kids don't understand what is happening. The parents assume that the children are so absorbed in their own world that they haven't time to focus on the difficulties between mom and dad. That is a wrong conclusion.

The offspring pick up on anger, bitterness, and estrangement much quicker than their parents realize. If all the family members are under the same roof, they are sensing the marital vibes, for better or worse. If Mom and Dad don't speak to each other civilly or they seldom touch or express warm affections, the kids notice. I've counseled situation in which the warring parents eventually decide to divorce. Then, one or both partners is stunned that the children say, "Thank God, they finally decided to go their separate ways. We wish they had done this sooner."

The longer that an irretrievable marriage continues its slow death, the more the children, caught in the middle, are open to satanic attack. Sometimes it is better for the kids to be with one loving parent than with two parents who hate each other. I always set out to save every marriage. That's the goal, but neither do I want to see offspring who are clinically depressed and even self-injurious because the rancor in the home led a child to the conclusion that he or she was the fault of the marriage being in crisis.

9. **Our marriage isn't** *that* **bad; we can still pull it out.** At the risk of sounding like a broken record, let me say again, every delay to get help is a death blow to the marriage. And let me reemphasize yet another point. When significant estrangement exists between spouses or parents and children, take decisive action. Most couples whom I counsel have gone past the tipping point of quick and easy solutions. In relationship dysfunction, things seldom just work themselves out, even with prayer and good intentions. It is my experience that a family in real crisis has systemic issues of malfunction that piety and prayer alone don't solve. The internal family systems need to be honestly examined and objective solutions offered.

Take the case where the kids are withdrawn and aloof. They seldom interact with Mom and Dad, except to exhibit rebellion. It's not enough to merely ship the kids off to Bible camp or demand that they spend certain minimum amounts of daily time reading the Bible. There may be peer influence the parents know nothing about. There could be serious spiritual oppression from generational family issues that haven't been confronted. Fatigue, hormone imbalances, delayed cognitive development, resentment from lack of parental involvement are just a few factors that may be in play. It often takes an outside person, even a mental health professional, to diagnose what's wrong.

Currently, our oldest daughter is studying to be a doctor. She works many hours in the emergency room assisting physicians as part of her preparation. She has remarked to us that many people who show up at the hospital are there too late. One particular case was a man who thought he was only having stomach pains from indigestion. Eventually, the discomfort was so great that family members insisted he go to the

E.R. Unfortunately, by the time he got there, the effects of a massive heart attack were in motion. Get the message?

It's a lot easier to set a family free when the internal dynamics of the marital relationship are only starting to get a little off course. It's not as hard to rescue a child on the verge of rebellious behavior as it is to pull back a kid who's gone over the edge with sex and drugs. In short, at the first sign of family deviation from desired Christian conduct, reach out for help. It's easier to stop a destructive individual from jumping off a cliff than it is to tenuously hold on to his arm as he dangles over the edge. Don't try to pull out a family situation after it has gone bad. Get the necessary help when you first sense that the Enemy has targeted those you love as part of a demonic assignment.

10. **Sex isn't that important.** I've met many couples who seem to think it is a virtue to abide in a nonsexual marriage, that they are putting spiritual priorities first and crucifying the flesh. Unless such persons are truly called to monasticism or a celibate single life, a sexless marriage is nothing to exalt. Usually one, or both partners, is living a lie, sublimating their needs and desires in the name of some larger good, like "crucifying the flesh."

There is a case to be made for sexless singleness. Paul does this in 1 Corinthians chapter seven. But before any sexless reader rides off on a holier-than-thou horse, remember that the context of Paul's admonitions about sexless singleness was based on the temper of the times, "this present distress" (verse 26). Paul was also honest enough to admit that he had "no commandment from the Lord" (verse 25) and was offering his perceptual wisdom.

This book isn't about the sexless single. Our focus is families, and that means sex is integral to normal emotional, and even spiritual, functioning. Unless there are reasonable medical reasons for foregoing sex, abstinence is usually not a measure of godliness. I've found that in many cases it is an excuse for the lack of intimate emotional connection. Married couples who are in love and are physically and emotionally healthy want to be intimate with each other. Satan is the one who wants the marriage bound by false ideas about marital sex being a condition of lesser spirituality. (See 1 Timothy 4:3 for an appraisal of this biblical aberration.)

There are seasons for celibacy. The apostle Paul speaks of this in 1 Corinthians 7:5. But such abstinence is scripturally appropriate only for a time and with mutual consent. In fact, Paul says that after such abstention, the married couple is to engage once again in intercourse, lest they become sexually tempted to sin. Make no mistake: Sex is an essential, permanent part of the marriage compact.

The Really Smart Thing

Don't do the dumb thing; do the really smart thing to set your family free. Heed carefully the advice this book has given. Our guidance is the result of intervention in the lives of thousands of people and many hundreds of troubled marriages. We've seen what doesn't work, and we know what does work. But don't take just our advice. Check out other credible Christian books on marriage and the family. Attend marriage seminars. Talk with your pastor about what you've read. Listen to seasoned Christian leaders who have successful marriages and families. Broaden your base of understanding beyond what may have been a less than successful marriage that your own parents suffered through. Talk to older, spiritually mature, couples about what has worked for them. Never stop learning and growing in your relationship with the Lord and with each other, and your children.

Chapter Six

INTENTIONAL DATING, MARRIAGE, AND PARENTING

When Bob and I first discussed writing this book, I knew that this was a chapter that I was very interested in. As a woman and mother, I've seen the sad results of nonintentional dating, marriage, and parenting. Intentionality puts things in the proper order: first dating, then marriage, with children to follow. When children are conceived and parenting comes before marriage, the relationship has limited chance for success. But this book is more than an attempt to encourage a return to traditional morality. Bob and I want your family to be truly *free,* and that is why intentions matter.

WHAT IS INTENTIONAL DATING, MARRIAGE, AND PARENTING?

Intentionality means being deliberate or purposeful, directing all of one's thoughts, beliefs, desires, and hopes toward some object or state of affairs.

Even the most intellectually and spiritually astute people fall in love, sip on the elixir of passion, and give no thought to what we're calling intentionality. Deep inside, most of us want to believe and partake in the happily-ever-after. Even the way we describe this wondrous feeling is revealing: We say we "fall" in love.

I understand this exuberance. I had similar feelings myself when I was engaged to my husband; however, even believing that God has brought us the right person does not negate our responsibility to God, potential mate, and future families to ask tough questions.

It's wise to seek counsel in all life's important decisions. But the time of life when marriage is being considered may be the most crucial. Bob and I have had many opportunities to counsel and spiritually guide couples who are contemplating marriage. Some have been newly engaged and others were still thinking about it. No one deliberately wants to marry the wrong person. But how are couples in love to know if they are foolishly saying "I do" when they should really be saying "no way?"

Couples who divorce often lament that they married the wrong person. But the chances of a dating couple figuring that out by themselves is slim. That's why our ministry offers a pre-engagement Encounter, hopefully to prevent the heartache of broken relationships.

At our first meeting with the couple, they are usually flooded with giddiness and excitement. They are dreaming of a life together, expressing their mutual affection abundantly. They can hardly take their eyes off each other. Some couples begin the session by saying that God brought them together. We hear declarations such as this: "I just knew that after I saw him the first time that he was the one." What they don't realize is that the blissful premarriage state may lure one or both of them to turn off logic and be overwhelmed with emotional conclusions.

Once they begin talking seriously about their time of dating, it's obvious that they have not bothered to look back to their lives before they met, and they have not peered forward very far into the future beyond the honeymoon. They often do not know much about each other's past or what specific plans they have for their lives ahead. Only a few couples have seriously discussed what their future will look like with children.

It is crucial to seek the perfect will of God. As part of doing that, every couple contemplating marriage must discover everything possible about their potential mate, and they must take an intentional approach to dating and marriage. That is, they must be deliberate and purposeful, and very few couples are. And it's best that this starts as soon as two individuals get serious about each other. It shouldn't be left to the time of intensive dating or the premarital period when a fixed wedding date has already been set.

Such objectivity is tough in the midst of that almost dream-like situation of being "in love." Asking each other really hard questions is to risk getting an answer you don't want to hear. No couple wants to rock the boat. Getting into a fight over something from the undisclosed past is a dream-dasher. It's unsettling to discover that one of the partners hopes for a big family while the other wants only a couple of kids. Such disclosures rock their world and send the giddy couple into depression. When a romance is moving full speed ahead, much is on the line. Emotions are running high. The good feelings are so intoxicating, and no one wants to cause any unnecessary problems or friction. People who are dating put on their very best faces, and they don't want to risk exposing a tarnished past life that would smear the image the lover holds dear.

What if you suddenly discover that the dream of your life has a detailed past involvement in the occult before finding Christ? If you're aware of spiritual warfare, even a little, you know that it can be problematic to fail to adequately break the curses of past witchcraft. Suppose your dream man or woman has been addicted to alcohol or drugs and hasn't been clean for very long, or worse, has not had adequate rehab intervention? Who, especially if there's already a ring on the finger and wedding invitations are being printed, wants to slow things down and take time for the addicted partner to get more professional help?

Intentionality seeks to set boundaries and benchmarks, which can help one evaluate how far into the relationship a couple should be. Intentionality makes it possible to reach conclusions based on hard facts, not starry eyes.

An Intentionality Case in Point

I remember so well one couple, Leslie and Luke, whose story makes clear the point I'm emphasizing. The day they came to our ministry, Luke was an absolute gentleman, holding the door for Leslie as she almost pirouetted into the office, excited to share with us about their engagement. They held each other's hands, and she beamed at him with her beautiful blue eyes. They were a sight to see, the perfect couple in their early twenties, he dark-haired and athletic, she a blonde dancer. He towered over her petite stature of 5'4" with his just over 6' tall frame. Luke looked protective of Leslie and made sure she got first pick of seats when they settled into the office chairs.

After a few introductory niceties, Leslie carefully put her purse under her chair, lifted her hand toward us in the air, and blurted out, "Isn't it beautiful? He asked me if I would marry him, and I said yes." Her eyes flashed at us with such pride and excitement, and she thrust her hand out to show us the dazzling ring. I jumped up and hugged her. Who wouldn't be overjoyed?

After a great time of exultation, the questions started flying. How had he proposed? When were they planning to get married? How far along were they in the planning details? Even as we focused on such positive elation, something in my spirit didn't seem right, but I didn't want to burst the bubble. They were there for a reason. They wanted to share their joy with us, but this meeting gave us an opportunity to ask bigger questions. Both Luke and Leslie had read Bob's books and knew about spiritual warfare. Yet nothing in their mutual flattery of each other hinted at any concern in this regard. "Why not?" I wondered.

I realized that at some point, we had to put pleasantries aside and cut to the chase. Fairy-tale love is heart-warming. I am a romantic, and I usually cheer for true love and the stuff of great movies. Inside I wanted to see this couple build their lives together, have a family and great future together, and ride off into the sunset. But after many years of sitting by Bob's side and watching him try to patch together broken lives five, ten, even twenty years after the "I do," I knew that I had to interject some reality into this happy setting. I most certainly didn't want this couple to come later needing ministry about serious problems. I didn't want them to ask, through tears and pain, "Why didn't you say something back then?"

That day, before the vows had yet been spoken, Bob and I had the opportunity to ask difficult questions. Luke and Leslie had to know if there were any hidden deal-breakers.

Fortunately, we were able to explore their pasts in detail and pray to break the curses of some very bad choices and toxic behavior from their families of origin. It was challenging for both of them to go through this prayer procedure. Neither wanted to bring up the garbage from the past and dump it into the middle of the good graces of their new relationship. This is typical of people who have fought past their damaged childhoods and the bad choices of their adult lives.

But here is what Bob and I have discovered over many years of helping people set their families free. If someone is entering a serious relationship that can lead to marriage, they don't need a partner to join them on the treadmill of life, adding the weight of even more problems. Instead, they need someone who is a spiritual equal who will constantly direct them to God and give them the strength to stay off that treadmill. Leslie and Luke understood this, and I was so proud of them. They were brave enough to set aside the great feelings that they shared together and take an honest look at each other's rough aspects. By doing this, they took a big step toward stopping the unhealthy patterns that came from having been raised in dysfunctional families. We have followed them since, and what they did that day in our office has paid off with a free family.

THE BLINDING HAZE OF LOVE

We've all heard of the "love haze," and part of it is truly physiological. When couples are in love, their hearts do beat faster. Their breath is shorter. Love affects both emotional and spiritual aspects of our beings. Falling in love is an amazing experience, one that most people hope for. It can feel like a once-in-a-lifetime thing, our guarantee of a happy ending in life. Love is the theme for plays, movies, and novels, and we cheer it on. On social media, people wildly "like" engagement photos. Elegant weddings are featured on sites like "The Knot." People throw extravagant parties to celebrate a couple's engagement. The momentum builds at every turn.

Too many couples push forward carelessly, wanting to avoid any downside to the relationship "high," especially the risk of emotional and spiritual pain that comes with breaking up. Breaking up really is "hard to do" and the thought of potential social rejection is devastating.

Some couples feel they could not go on without the other and they can get downright angry toward people who would dare burst the bubble and say anything negative about where the relationship is headed! But when we're in a situation bigger than ourselves, we must seek the guidance of the Lord. And often He speaks to us through parents, loved ones, and trusted friends. He will warn us and guide us even if it means canceling or delaying a marriage.

It takes enormous trust on behalf of an engaged couple to allow anyone into their world of emotional intimacy. If you are anticipating marriage, remember that God can use highly trusted people to be sounding boards during this time when your emotional equilibrium may be a bit off balance.

In advocating intentional dating and preparation for marriage, we must never forget that the love haze can make us vulnerable during this time and can even blind us to red flags. We must not ignore a sense of divine hesitation about potential problems in a relationship. As we all know from witnessing divorce and broken homes, it is better for a couple to figure out the nitty-gritty about one another before their wedding than later on when their lives are deeply intertwined, with children.

Don't think you're too spiritual to be deceived. Some people who seek our help about a relationship are very astute about spiritual warfare. These individuals know about the potential attacks of Satan. They understand how to combat demonic forces, how to pray, what spiritual strongholds to avoid, and what might allow sinister demonic openings in their lives. They may even serve as ministers themselves and help others steer clear from the clutches of potentially dangerous soul-connections. But when it comes to their own deep emotional involvement, they are blind, blind, blind.

They can blow off sound advice and say, "Yeah, yeah, we get it, but what you're saying applies to everyone else, not us. We love each other and we've prayed about it." Please know that playing the God-card is unwise, especially when other mature Christians are suggesting caution.

It can happen to the best of us, because love makes even godly people vulnerable. Having created a fantasy world where everything is rose-colored and wishing to perpetuate the love story at all costs, it seems incomprehensible that an attack of the enemy can come wrapped in the form of a lovely person, someone who has stolen our heart. We forget that demons do not come walking up to humans and tap them on the shoulder before leveling them. Instead, demons exploit and invade the human soul, worming their way in to cause mayhem, harm, and evil to the host. That does not imply that your beloved is in the enemy camp. But he or she may come with a spiritual agenda, likely hidden from view, that may bring down a happy marriage.

I did use the D word (demon) in the previous paragraph—in the context of love and marriage. Although evil spirits don't seem to fit with love stories, there is often a dangerous connection. The devil wants every love story rewritten into a tragedy. Bob and I see it often, heartbreaking stories about "perfect" couples who after a few years of marriage descend into misery and are on the verge of splitting up. After the nuptials, they found out about the "dark side" of the person they married, and now they feel bitter about being duped by the love of their life.

Do you see why we encourage intentional preparation for marriage that exposes problem areas before the knot is tied?

WHAT IS A COUPLE TO DO?

Here is a checklist of things to consider if you feel that your heart is being drawn romantically to another person. I've broken this down into sections that I pray will help you to better understand each phase of the progression from attraction to marriage to parenting.

Intentional predating. As we discuss elsewhere in this book, every adolescent should be properly prepared with as deep an understanding as possible of sexuality, dating, engagement, and marriage. Nothing should be left to the imagination. Every question should be answered. Every possibility considered. Parents need to have open and transparent communication with their young adults about what to look for in a love interest.

Parents, it's all right to be very specific about the kind of mate you want for your child. We're not suggesting anything bordering on arranged marriages, but you should clearly articulate your preferences about the kind of person you believe will make your child happy.

For starters, a life partner must share your child's faith in Christ. It's also helpful if the prospective mate comes from a similar theological background. Socioeconomic factors should be discussed. These are not things you throw on the table in the first few dates. But as the couple gets to know each other, even before spending time alone together, they should both be noticing any signs of incompatibility that might pose difficult hurdles to get over. The young person embarking on this adventure of romance should develop a mental list of nonnegotiable factors that will automatically eliminate certain individuals.

Intentional predating also includes an adequate understanding of sexual development and an introduction to the world of "me-boy, you-girl" attraction that makes the world go 'round.

Intentional dating. This is the time to get to know yourself and the person you are interested in. It doesn't have to be heart-throbbing. In fact, it's healthier to move into the idea of sexual attraction gradually. But in the back of your mind, you are always thinking about what this person's life was like before you met them, and how that will fit into the way you were raised spiritually, socially, even economically.

If you're born in the Bronx, you may have serious challenges living with someone who wants to settle on a rural farm in Georgia. If you are pursuing a graduate degree, dinner table conversation might be difficult if your mate went straight to employment after high school. If you were raised in a liturgical church, are you prepared to worship with a mate who was born into a hardcore Pentecostal family? These and other similar questions may not seem relevant when you are basking in the glow of new love, but if you marry, you'll have to live a quite normal life with this person you are so infatuated with. Just make certain that your mutual histories and future desires are compatible.

Intentional dating means taking off the rose-tinted glasses and considering the hard facts of compatibility for the long haul. Is the person you're dating someone to whom you'd want to wake up next to each day?

Intentional engagement. If you are at this stage and haven't known to heed the "intentional" teachings of this book, get busy before it becomes difficult to turn back the clock on your relational involvement. *Do not* set a date (or postpone it if one has been set) until you've carefully considered the warnings of this book. The momentum of an engagement is driven by hormones, the pressure of family and friends, and your own compulsion to get things over with and move on to wedded bliss. A wise person will practice due diligence before buying a house. They may have it inspected. Talk to former owners. Hire a lawyer to go over the contract. Make sure the real estate agent has checked for bankruptcy status or other encumbrances. Prospective buyers may walk through the house many times, checking every faucet and handle. Such care and concern is seldom applied to a potential mate. We study a manual to learn how to drive a car, but often follow only our hearts when it comes to navigating romantic relationships.

Premarital counseling is all-important. Many excellent Christian books give valuable guidelines regarding marriage. One of the best is *How to Get Engaged,* written by Christian leadership expert Bobb Biehl.[4] (We not only read the book. Bobb was Bob's best man at our wedding!) Study to "show yourself approved," as Scripture says.

Intentional engagement means never having to say you're sorry after the wedding bells.

Intentional marriage. Marriage isn't a journey of ecstasy. It's a commitment to love someone and show it by actions. But in the process, you will learn the hardest task for which God created us: loving and living in respectful relationship with another human being. If it's truly a godly relationship, you will be more emotionally and sexually bonded to them every day. Intentional marriage is living each day with the one you love and learning more every hour how to meet their needs at a heartfelt level.

Intentional marriage doesn't begin with the cutting of the wedding cake or the honeymoon. It plays out over the entire process of meeting and getting to know the person with whom you'll share your deepest secrets and most fragile emotions. Intentionally get to know everything possible about the person you'll be sleeping next to every night and baring your soul to day after day. Ask specific questions. Here are some samples that provoke discussion beyond, "What's your favorite color?" or "What kinds of music do you like best?" These suggestions are not exhaustive, but designed to get the reader thinking about their own list of most important inquiries to ask a possible marriage mate.

- What do you dislike the most in a person if you're around them 24/7?

- Do you have any habits that a mate might find strange or offensive?

- Did you plan on having a family? How many children would be ideal?

- How clearly defined is your biblical understanding of the role sex plays in marriage?

- What about your parents' relationship did you most admire? Most dislike?

- What sort of church are you most comfortable attending?

- Who do you think should be in charge of finances?

- Should personal assets be kept separate or comingled?

- How harsh was the disciplinary style in your parent's home?

And then, here are really specific questions about spiritual life:

- What do you think helps most to keep a strong spiritual faith?

- What are your current prayer and Bible reading disciplines?

- How important is it to be involved in church activities?

- What is your understanding of breaking family curses?

- Have you experienced the need for deliverance and acted upon it?

- Have you ever talked to a Christian counselor or therapist about personal issues?

- Do you have any addictions that you're still struggling with?

- What priority do you place on a prayer relationship with your spouse?

- What sins or spiritual struggles have been most damaging in your family?

- What's the worst thing that's happened to you and have you healed from it?

As you can readily see, our idea of intentional marriage leaves as little to the imagination as possible. Keep in mind that some questions would be best posed by a pastor or counseling professional. But if you are contemplating marriage, be certain that you've asked the Holy Spirit to guide you with your own checklist of things that are important to know before signing that marriage license.

Intentional parenting. It's been said that nothing can prepare you for parenting. Amen. But that doesn't mean that you shouldn't anticipate the responsibility well in advance of getting pregnant. Here are some things that indicate intentionality: the decision regarding how soon to have children after getting married; reaching agreement on how large a family you both desire; whether or not you have applied the excellent advice that is available in Christian books about parenting and the family.

Parenting changes a lot of things in a marital relationship. Sexual patterns are altered. Sleep deprivation is high. A couple's private time together is challenged. Financial practices are altered. Leisure time takes a hit. Of course, these challenges are far outweighed by the joy of welcoming one of God's most precious gifts, a newborn child. But it's not all coos and giggles. The better two new parents are prepared for the vexations of parenthood, the smoother the process of family multiplication will be.

All the ins and outs of being a parent have been adequately addressed by a large number of excellent Christian books already on the shelves. Read them. Our encouragement here is to not wait until you are pregnant to start getting educated about this most serious of life's responsibilities. Before marriage, during the engagement, soon after the ceremony, begin preparations for being a parent. Once that umbilical cord is cut, it may be a little late to consider all that parenting entails.

ENDNOTE

1. Available at http://bobbbiehl.com/product/how-to-get-engaged.

Chapter Seven

CURSING AND BLESSING YOUR CHILDREN

Bob and I had the opportunity to minister to a lovely, deeply devoted Christian woman named Linda who felt it was time to break curses over her life. She had heard about the ministry and believed that our teachings about curse-breaking held the answer to her prayers for relief from torment. Linda faithfully sought the Lord and asked Him to give her peace about seeking inner healing and deliverance. After reaching out to us, she scheduled four ministry Encounter sessions in various cities where Bob conducted seminars. The fifth Encounter was at our Spiritual Freedom Center in Phoenix, Arizona.

It was Christmastime, and Linda wanted to give herself a gift that was made possible because of Jesus' gift when he took her curses on the cross. She said she had felt so much better after receiving ministry during the previous four sessions and her family and friends had seen a dramatic difference.

We don't usually allow time for Encounter sessions right before Christmas because it is our family time, but we knew she needed help. In spite of the wonderful progress that she had made, Linda still experienced extreme torment, even though she had called on Christ to be her Lord and Savior. Her life was in a near-constant state of agitation and anxiety. She was being attacked in almost every area, both physically and mentally, and knew that she had to get help right away. (Situations like this are common in the early stages of the deliverance process; great strides forward can be taken, but Satan puts up one final intensive battle to hold the little territory that he has left.) She flew to Phoenix with the stated intention of dealing with any unbroken curses in her life.

I was astounded when I first met her, because she wasn't what I expected. This forty-something mother of a teenage son looked like she had it altogether. Beautiful and accomplished, she gave no outward signs of inner torment. She knew differently, however, that her issues were deep and powerful. With a humble heart, she had reached out for help. Linda was like so many individuals that Bob and I have met. Even after giving her heart to Christ and serving him faithfully for many years, she still felt afflicted by the enemy. Along with being distressed, she was also embarrassed by what was going on spiritually in her life. She struggled deep inside with issues that no one knew about. A secret curse seemed to have been inflicted upon her as a child, and she felt she was destined to suffer in silence or risk being judged.

As a mother, I identified with her pain and felt so sad for what she had been through, always trying to do the right thing but not finding the help she needed until now. Linda's session of ministry with us was a dramatic time of inner healing, curse-breaking, and intensive exorcism. When it was all over, she was radiant and greatly relieved. Without hesitation, she told us that her Encounter session was the best investment she had ever made. As so many who've received similar help, Linda said that she felt as though a huge weight had been lifted from her. Now she no longer had to live in fear of the childhood memory of being abused by a family member. The secret was out, the curse was broken, and she was finally free.

Best of all, Linda was also able to break the power of this incestuous curse over her teenage son, freeing him from potential harm before he became an adult. So far, she didn't know any violations that he had suffered. But she understood that Satan was surely bidding his time to strike at a demonically opportune moment. Now the devil's plan had been shattered and Linda had been able to rid herself of her own curses. "This was the best day of my life," Linda said as she left.

I understood how her mother's heart felt. Bob and I have broken off every curse we would suspect that might spiritually hinder our children. Some were obvious to us, like alcohol and addiction from my father's family line and the same curse from Bob's side. We have learned the importance of breaking bloodline curses not only for our own sake but for the sake of our children—preferably before we turn them loose into a fallen, sin-filled world.

MUST CURSES BE BROKEN FROM CHRISTIAN CHILDREN?

You might ask, "Do you really need to break curses over children? Doesn't salvation solve it?" In Bob's book *Curse Breaking* he deals with this question in great scriptural detail. It is a book that, as a parent, you simply can't be without. Here is a portion taken from page 22 of Bob's book, the section entitled, "Christ, Cursed for You and Me":

> The Bible tells us clearly that Jesus Christ was made a curse for us. People who don't like to hear a message such as mine often choose to quote Paul's words: "Christ has redeemed us from the curse of the law, having become a curse for us (for it is written, 'Cursed is everyone who hangs on a tree')" (Gal. 3:13, quoting Deut. 21:23). They consider Christ's sacrifice on the cross to be the blanket solution to all curses and they say that everything related to curse-breaking is a bunch of bunk.

121

Such people confuse positional truth with conditional reality. The positional truth is that, yes, Jesus Christ was cursed for us, and yes, He bore the curse of sin to the cross, and yes, because of his resurrection victory over death, we ought to be free from every curse. But like every promise in the Word of God, this one is of no effect until you believe it, receive it, and appropriate it by faith. The Good News is powerful. The bad news is that it is not automatic. Each person needs to appropriate the blessing of salvation as it applies to the realities of his or her own life.

Through many years of ministry, we've witnessed many young people who have received the blessings of their parent's spiritual covering and assume that it will continue in perpetuity. They enjoy the blessing of their parents' godly lives, as it says in Psalm 119:2 (NIV), "Blessed are those who keep his statutes and seek him with all their heart."

It is true that the spiritual covering of parents includes their children. Unbroken curses may not even land on a child until the age of eighteen, which we'll discuss in the next chapter. But one of the important lessons that Bob and I have learned in many years of deliverance ministry is this: Take no chances with the possibility of family bloodline curses. It is best to break all curses before the enemy has a chance to set up a stronghold in the lives of children in order to attack after they become adults.

ABOUT CURSES

It is important to understand what a curse is and how it happens. I want to be certain that each reader fully understands the impact that family curses may have if they are not renounced. Here's what the *International Standard Bible Encyclopedia* says about curses:

CURSES: (*'alah* (Numbers 5:21,23,17, etc.), *me'erah* (Proverbs 3:33; Malachi 2:2, etc.), *klalah* (Genesis 27:12,13);

katara (Galatians 3:10,13)): This word as noun and verb renders different Hebrew words, some of them being more or less synonymous, differing only in degree of strength. It is often used in contrast with "bless" or "blessing" (Deuteronomy 11:29). When a curse is pronounced against any person, we are not to understand this as a mere wish, however violent, that disaster should overtake the person in question, any more than we are to understand that a corresponding "blessing" conveys simply a wish that prosperity should be the lot of the person on whom the blessing is invoked. A curse was considered to possess an inherent power of carrying itself into effect.

I refer again to my husband's book, *Curse Breaking,* which has many wonderful prayers for families and individuals. I would highly recommend it for people who want to do the very best for their children because Bob reveals critical facts about the nature and types of curses and how to break them.

Curses are caused by sin in many forms and advance the enemy's plan to kill, steal, and destroy (see John 10:10). Curses can cause habitual sin, misery, pain and torment, shame, sickness, mental illness, and even death. We all need to break curses over ourselves, our spouses, our minor children, and future grandchildren.

A Personal Example of Curse-Breaking

In my life, I have had to break the curse of addiction due to my father's desire for alcohol, which he loved more than anything. We know from empirical, statistical evidence that those who have a family history of alcoholism have a higher risk of developing a drinking problem. Studies show that at least 50 percent of the predisposition toward alcoholism comes from genetics.[5] Spiritually, alcoholism can also be a curse that needs to be broken off the family bloodline. For me, it was as simple as commanding all the evil spirits of addiction and alcoholism to be removed from my bloodline and future generations. Done!

CRUCIAL FACTS ABOUT CURSES AND BLESSINGS

Let me suggest several areas of your child's life you might consider addressing. What I share below isn't exhaustive, but perhaps it will alert you to some curses that you haven't considered.

To start with, inspect the spiritual evil you know exists in your family history. As an example, I previously mentioned the addictive tendencies in my bloodline. Some of the sins and curses you might encounter in your family history may be far more sinister. Ask pertinent questions of living, elderly family members about your bloodline. Do the same about your mate's. Was anyone a known adulterer, deceiver, con man? Was anyone guilty of a crime of moral turpitude?

The Legal Dictionary states that moral turpitude refers generally to conduct that shocks the public conscience as being inherently base, vile, or depraved, contrary to the rules of morality and social duty. A person commits a crime of moral turpitude out of either evil intent or recklessness. Some examples of deviant and degenerate crimes are as follows: murder, voluntary manslaughter, involuntary manslaughter, rape, spousal abuse, child abuse, incest, kidnapping, robbery, aggravated assault, mayhem, animal fighting, theft, fraud, conspiracy attempt, or acting as an accessory to a crime if that crime involved moral turpitude.

Consider other negative patterns in your families of origin such as mental illness, poverty, divorce, accidents, hauntings, sudden death, and a wide array of health issues. Flag all known, repeated problems in your ancestral line as potential pitfalls and make your child aware of them, as it is appropriate.

Then seek help to break any pattern of sin or crime that has plagued your bloodline so that these evils can be stopped now, before your child is on his or her own.

IF YOU WEREN'T A CHRISTIAN FOR PART OF YOUR CHILD'S LIFE

If you were not a Christian for most of the time your children were young, consider behaviors that you may have modeled to your children which were contrary to your present convictions and faith. Your sinful and rebellious behavior may have incurred curses, even though now you are a new spiritual creation in Christ (see 2 Corinthians 5:17).

To keep your children from following in your footsteps, you can break those curses on yourself and your children. You can be honest and share with your children what it meant to be a non-Christian and how much Christ has changed your life. Most children can see the difference in your life and will be relieved to hear you talk about it and give credit to Christ for the change. It is helpful to explain that we are all a work in progress, and that with God's help you will continue to sanctify your life. Be as honest as possible if you think much damage has been done. In addition, you might have your child talk with a Christian counselor if they need to deal with some of the challenges of their own unsaved childhood. The earlier a child can come to understand their internal lives, the better.

Consider these few Scripture verses as an example of possible generational curses that you will want to have removed from your child:

These six things the Lord hates, yes, seven are an abomination to Him:
A proud look,
A lying tongue,
Hands that shed innocent blood,
A heart that devises wicked plans,
Feet that are swift in running to evil,
A false witness who speaks lies,
And one who sows discord among brethren. (Proverbs 6:16-19)

If you know of anyone in your family bloodline who has behaved like this, start breaking curses now! Also, consider the words of Micah: "Woe to those who devise wickedness and work evil on their beds! When the morning dawns, they perform it, because it is in the power of their hand" (Micah 2:1, ESV). How many of us have had ancestors who thought and acted like this? Although you may not be able to trace your ancestry back to such evil directly, you can certainly ask the Holy Spirit to cleanse your bloodline of all the iniquities that have contributed to your genetic identity.

Be honest with your child. Make certain your child knows that even in Christian homes there can be toxic behavior and that, despite the family faults and failures, there are moral standards for their behavior, standards that are not subjective, but rather built upon the teachings of the Bible. Clear up gray areas in family life and establish ongoing criteria of behavior that will be healthy for everyone.

How to Break the Curses You've Spoken over Your Children

What if you said emotionally damaging things to your children when you were less mature in the Lord? Sometimes we carelessly label and curse our children, for example: "I wish you had never been born." "I must have been drunk when I made you." "You are a blight on this world and the cause of all of my problems." "You will never amount to anything." "You are just like _____ (a relative who is considered a loser)."

If you have said negative or evil things to your children in anger, ask your children for forgiveness! Ask them if you have said anything that has hurt them and reverse what you spoke over their lives. It may hurt to hear how much you wounded them, but if you want them to be healed, it is worth the emotional pain.

If you are still guilty of speaking unwise words to your children, change your heart and ask God to fill you with His love. Don't let the enemy use you to inflict any more damage on your child. Instead of cursing, bless. Ask God to show you the good qualities in your children. He made them, and there's much good in His beautiful creation; speak to your children about that instead of railing on them. As you speak to each child about the good that is in him or her, don't offer cheap compliments. Express authentic, uncontrived praise. (They will spot disingenuousness immediately.) Tell them how much you love them, and mean it!

HOW TO TURN CURSES INTO BLESSINGS

Blessings that parents pass on to their children are a powerful spiritual force. In the Old Testament, blessings were important ways to transfer family leadership from one generation to the next, as with Abraham and Isaac, Isaac and Jacob. In that light, you may want to consider a special prayer time when your child becomes an adolescent or right before they turn eighteen, as we'll discuss in the next chapter.

Many times, I have watched Bob declare a prayer of blessing over a male child. This is especially important when that child has been abandoned by his father or abused by his parents in some way. This prayer has a spiritually rejuvenating effect. He lays his hands on the boy's head and utters words like these:

_____ (inserting the child's name), as an earthly father and as a man of God representing your Father in heaven, I bless you with the blessing of a father. I bless you in your going out and your coming in; in your leisure and your labor. I bless your hopes, your dreams, and your destiny. I bless who you are and who you desire to be. I bless the purpose for which God created you. And in blessing you, I cancel every curse that the devil has placed on your life. I also cancel every assignment of Satan to hinder the fulfillment of your spiritual gifts. As a father, I bless you, I bless you, I bless you.

When Bob does this, I watch in amazement as the young man receiving the prayer undergoes a miraculous transformation. Tears flow where there was only coldness of heart before. Smiles replace depression. Often after the prayer time, the young man leaves a totally changed person. Something supernatural has happened; an unseen alteration in the spiritual realm has taken place. While others may have hurt and cursed him before, Bob has stepped forward to bless and invoke the favor of God.

As a mother, I have also spoken similar blessings over young women. My prayer formula is somewhat like Bob's, but it includes my own special instincts as a mother of three daughters. Here is my prayer of blessing:

> _____ (inserting the girl child's name), is a gift from you, Lord, and I thank you, Father, for her. Let her walk in the authority of your assigned worth to her. Let her always obey you, Lord and find joy in your precepts. Let her remain under your wing and your protective covering. Give her boldness, courage and strength in you. May she be blessed all the days of her life. Help her to recognize sin traps and flee immediately. As a mother, I speak the love of God into her very being, and I ask the Father to fill her life with blessings and honor.

A FINAL WORD ABOUT THE POWER OF BLESSINGS AND CURSING

It is so important to understand how to put an end to painful curses that have lingered for years over your family. It takes a humble and willing spirit to look pain and sin in the face, to see the enemy's plans behind it, and to draw a line. Truth and forgiveness pave the way to freedom. Eliminate family curses, those vehicles for pain, so that they won't travel on the next generation. Do your very best for your children by recognizing curses and aggressively breaking them before your child's entry into adulthood. Agree that all family curses stop here and now! Take action in Jesus' name! Hallelujah.

ENDNOTE

1. "Our genetic structure determines all of our human traits. Our DNA dictates our physical characteristics, such as eye color and also our behavior characteristics, such as aggression. These genes are passed on to us by our parents. Among the behavioral traits parents can pass on to their children is a predisposition toward alcohol abuse and addiction. Among those abusing alcohol, people who are genetically predisposed to alcoholism have a higher risk of becoming addicted. Although people can inherit alcoholic tendencies, the development of an alcohol use disorder is also dependent on social factors. Some who have inherited genes making them susceptible to alcoholism are responsible drinkers or never take a drink in their life." (www.AddictionCenter.com)

Chapter Eight

SET YOUR CHILDREN FREE AT EIGHTEEN

Not long ago, our daughter Brooke, the brunette beauty, celebrated her eighteenth birthday. It was a big event for our entire family. We pulled out all the stops on her celebration, which was made possible by an enthusiastic group of friends and family; her sisters, grandmother, and I spent hours planning to organize a true surprise, which she is still talking about.

We felt it was important to properly commemorate this once-in-a-lifetime passage into adulthood, so one half of her birthday observance included a party and the other half involved a unique get-together with just Brooke, Bob, and me on the day before the party. The party was not lavish, but it was filled with many friends and a rich outpouring of love.

Laura's Perspective as a Mother

We had work to do before this important birthday, and I don't mean all the party-planning and invitation-sending. Bob and I had to plan for Brooke's spiritual health for the rest of her life. We knew what we needed to do. We'd been down this path before, thanks to our radiant redhead Brynne, who had turned eighteen three years earlier.

For our children, the eighteenth birthday is significant. From their birth onward, Bob and I have given to our children every ounce of energy and love that we could offer. I wish I could say we were perfect, but we did the best that we could through prayer and example. The most important thing that Bob and I could offer Brooke was a desire to serve the Lord. As a mother, I prayed daily for her and her relationship with God. I also focused on her future life, awaiting the day that she would become an adult.

The day before the eighteenth birthdays of both Brynne and Brooke, we met with them to break any curses on their lives. As parents, still having authority over them before the legal age of enfranchisement, we renounced on their behalf any spiritually legal rights that the Enemy might claim to their lives. We considered our own family as well as the known ancestors in both our bloodlines. We prayed over any areas where we saw potential problems or inherited evil. We considered behavioral, health, and spiritual issues.

Our children had always been protected by our prayers, but one more time we wanted to confront any demonic spiritual assignments while we, as parents, were still accountable for them. For Brooke, as it had been with Brynne three years before, that eighteenth birthday would change everything. The laws of our land would now perceive her differently, and henceforth she would be held accountable for her own spiritual choices as well. We could, one final time, legally intercede for her as her sole spiritual covering.

Spiritual Accountability of Adulthood

Accountability is defined in a legal sense as "the state of being liable, answerable, or accountable." That means that some legal rule exists under which a claim can be made to find one liable in a civil law suit or culpable in a criminal matter. Under state laws, a person must reach a certain age before they can be held accountable in both civil and criminal matters. That age is known as the age of majority. In most states the age is eighteen and in a few it is nineteen. In our state, eighteen is the age of majority; from Brooke's eighteenth birthday onward, she would be accountable as an adult in the eyes of the law.

It makes sense that spiritual laws would follow the legal system which determines that a person becomes accountable for themselves at a certain age, although most parents haven't been taught anything about it. Scripture puts it this way: Romans 13:1 (NLT), *"Everyone must submit to governing authorities. For all authority comes from God, and those in positions of authority have been placed there by God."* And: *"Therefore, each of us will give an account of himself to God"* (Romans 14:12, net).

Bob and I believe that the spiritual age of majority follows the legal age of majority as designated by the law of the land. That doesn't mean that we as parents could not help or pray for our daughters any longer, but it's different after age eighteen, when a child is considered an adult who is accountable both legally and spiritually. From a prayerful perspective, it means that the strongest prayers would come directly from her. Certainly, we continue to pray for both Brooke and Brynne, but they as adults now have the legal right to pray as they see fit, and we no longer could pray in their stead.

Sometimes parents with adult children will ask if they can break curses over their adult children, even against their will. The technical answer is, "No." The most effective prayer is for legal adults to pray for themselves. Once a child has been emancipated, the parent can no longer speak for them in a legal sense. (As we've explained, this also applies spiritually.) It's also important to engage, as much as possible, the will of a child when praying over them. Prayer for a minor child will be more effective if that son or daughter is able to morally perceive the purpose of the prayer and stand in agreement with the parent.

How did we get ready for Brooke's pre-eighteenth-birthday curse-breaking get-together? It really took eighteen years of what we've already described as "intentional parenting." This is parenting with the full intent to prepare your child for life and adulthood. As children are growing up, time passes quickly and it seems like a sprint requiring a lot of prayer, study, hard work, dedication, patience, forgiveness, and love. It may seem like childhood will last forever, but, as they say, "in the blink of an eye it is over." On that eighteenth birthday, you may want to delay the reality of knowing that your baby is now an adult, but you can't put off time. We encourage you to do what Bob and I have done. Plan and take adequate time to prepare your child for that last get-together when you'll have your last prayer while he or she is still under your total spiritual covering. In addition to praying curse-breaking prayers, ask your young adult if there is anything you can pray in agreement over; address in prayer any areas of adulthood that may be causing fear or apprehension. Encourage your son or daughter to take up the mantle of adulthood with all of its benefits, responsibilities, and accountability. This is not another childhood birthday party, but a life-changing turning point in their lives. Along with your love, advice, and support, launch your child into adulthood by giving the gift of *freedom*.

Before your child's eighteenth birthday, you should have been praying to break off any assignments, curses, or legal rights the enemy may claim to your child. (You will find sample prayers in chapter twelve.) Start preparing to pray such prayers now, even if you are the parent of a baby in the crib. Prepare your children to give it everything they have to create a strong relationship with the Lord, with the goal of living an independent adult life, free from Satan's curses and demonic legal rights and responsible for growing their own spiritual life.

When we met with Brooke that day we went even further in our prayers. We asked the Lord to remove every unknown malediction that had been genetically embedded in our ancestors. God alone knows what potential harm to Brooke was averted that day. What we do know is that we took seriously the words of Exodus 34:7, "Keeping mercy for thousands, forgiving iniquity and transgression and sin, by no means clearing the guilty; visiting the iniquity of the fathers upon the children and the children's children, to the third and to the fourth generation."

Always remember that curses remain in place if left unbroken and they risk sabotaging a person for the rest of their lives. Parents must address these generational evils before the age of majority. You might say, "Of course I would not want a curse to fall on any of my children." Perhaps you have had firsthand experiences with curses and do not want such sad circumstances to befall your children. But the point I can't emphasis enough is that, unless you take deliberate action against bloodline maladies, your children could become unwitting victims once they are gone from you and are on their own.

PREPARING FOR THE ONCE-IN-A-LIFETIME MEETING

Each family will have its own idea about how to handle this important occasion. The suggestions below are based on what Bob and I have done. Our planning for our meeting the day before an eighteenth birthday accommodates these basic points:

1. We tell our daughter what will happen a few weeks ahead of the proposed day. We encourage her to pray and seek the Lord's wisdom regarding what she wants out of this meeting. We asked her to think of any specific areas that she would like prayer for and to contemplate what adulthood will mean to her.

2. The designated day, as explained above, is the day before the eighteenth birthday. It is better to meet earlier in the day rather than later. If you must meet some time before that last day of age seventeen, try to make it as close to the actual birthday as possible. Don't let the scheduling create undue stress and cause a hurried or rushed attitude. Your intentionality and care will show how much you value this moment in time.

3. Create a calm, quiet, private environment, where you will not be interrupted. You want your child to understand the importance of the meeting and feel safe to share questions and concerns. Pray and bless the area where you will have your time together.

4. Plan approximately an hour for this meeting.

5. Start out with a prayer and ask God to lead in every area of this time together. Take charge of the proceedings spiritually. Bind any intrusion by Satan to disrupt or steal the time, and ask for the Holy Spirit's guidance.

6. Talk about what it means to be an adult, legally, practically, and spiritually. Define adulthood, both legally and spiritually. Explain that adulthood is a daunting challenge. Hopefully, this won't be your first conversation about this rite of passage.

7. Conclude with the Prayer Before a Child Becomes a Legal Adult, which you will find in chapter twelve of this book.

Important Points to Make During Your Coming-of-Age Discussion

The points for consideration below follow the template that we have laid out for our own children:

1. Legal considerations: Explain the way that the law views a person who has reached the age of majority, that there are new rights and responsibilities associated with being independent, and adults are held personally accountable for their actions in society and in the eyes of the law. Point out that the age of eighteen (in most states) is the moment when each child is automatically given all the rights of an adult. Tell your child that you will honor these rights. An exception in our case, as a matter of family standards, is to forgo the freedom to consume alcoholic beverages. In most states the rights of adulthood include, but are not limited to, the following:

- Voting
- Making a will and exercising power of attorney
- Making end-of-life decisions
- Becoming an organ donor
- Signing a contract (to rent an apartment, buy a car, take out a loan) in one's own name
- Obtaining medical treatment without parental consent
- Enlisting in the armed forces without parental consent
- Being completely independent from parental control
- Applying for credit
- Becoming legally married

2. Responsibilities with serious consequences: What are some of the consequences that ensue with coming of age?

- People who break the law will be tried in adult criminal court rather than juvenile court.
- Parents are no longer required to support and provide their children.
- People may be sued by others regarding contracts or binding agreements that they have entered into.
- Registered voters and/or licensed drivers are eligible for jury duty.
- All males must register with Selective Service.

3. Practically speaking, what does this mean? In a nutshell, adults are entirely accountable for their actions and their behavior must support these adult responsibilities. Adult privileges are great, if a person is responsible enough to make wise choices. These choices run the gamut from the serious to the practical. For some, this may mean saying no to drugs. To others, not getting a puppy until they can take care of it properly.

4. Spiritually speaking, what does this mean? The Bible supports this concept of an adult threshold. Consider this Scripture: "When I was a child, I spoke like a child, I thought like a child, I reasoned like a child. When I became a man, I gave up childish ways" (1 Corinthians 13:11, ESV).

Spiritual decisions have weightier consequences. No longer does a child enjoy the spiritual covering of parents. The child of godly parents will continue into adulthood to receive spiritual generational blessings. But unrepented sin in adulthood can rob those blessings as documented in the Old Testament. For example, Solomon initially walked in the blessings of David: "He said to me, 'It is Solomon your son who shall build my house and my courts'" (1 Chronicles 28:6, ESV). Keeping a blessing and building upon it is part of responsible independence. Solomon had a blessed start and was honored to build the temple. But as we know from the story of his life, Solomon veered off course and failed to obey the Lord faithfully. Consequently, his life's work was summed in Ecclesiastes 2:20: "So I began to despair about all the fruit of my labor for which I worked so hard on earth" (NET).

Your child will need to fight his or her own spiritual battles: "We do not wrestle against flesh and blood, but against the rulers, against the authorities, against the cosmic powers over this present darkness, against the spiritual forces of evil in the heavenly places" (Ephesians 6:12, ESV).

Hopefully, your children will have prayer support from your church family and extended family; but they need to realize that they personally must develop a vigilance against the enemy, in accordance with Peter's advice in Scripture: "Be sober, be vigilant; because your adversary the devil walks about like a roaring lion, seeking whom he may devour" (1 Peter 5:8). When you understand spiritual warfare, you know that these Scriptures should not make you fearful but rather emboldened with the wisdom and authority in Christ to be on guard.

Also remind your child of Christ's admonition: "Watch and pray that you may not enter into temptation. The spirit indeed is willing, but the flesh is weak" (Matthew 26:41, ESV). Remind your child that no one is beyond temptation and that he or she will now join the ranks of Christian adults who battle the enemy as the Body of Christ. Remind your child how easy it is for seemingly astute people to get tripped up by the enemy, if not destroyed.

Point out to your child the good news that their lives will be blessed if they follow the Lord according to Ephesians 3:1: "The God and Father of our Lord Jesus Christ...has blessed us in Christ with every spiritual blessing in the heavenly places." Tell your child how to walk in blessings and not curses.

Last, but certainly not least, give your child a sense of mission as they enter the world of being an adult. I especially like the biblical passage that footnotes our ministry, Luke 4:18: "The Spirit of the Lord is upon me, because he has anointed me to proclaim good news to the poor. He has sent me to proclaim release to the captives and the regaining of sight to the blind, to set free those who are oppressed" (NET). Freedom is given through Christ, but it is an active state of being. Typically, the more people help others attain freedom, the more they keep theirs.

COMING-OF-AGE CURSE-BREAKING

In the previous chapter, we mentioned Galatians 3:13–14, which declares that "Christ has redeemed us from the curse of the law, having become a curse for us (for it is written, 'Cursed is everyone who hangs on a tree'), that the blessing of Abraham might come upon the Gentiles in Christ Jesus, that we might receive the promise of the Spirit through faith." With that Scripture to establish the right to break curses, it's now time to claim your parental authority one final time. Let the curse-breaking begin. To get started, here are some areas in which to break curses:

1. Take a broad approach to start by renouncing all generational curses and iniquities resulting from the sins of ancestors.

2. Break all curses on both bloodlines, all the way back to Adam and Eve.

3. Break all witchcraft, divination, and sorcery curses in Jesus' name.

4. Break all curses to reject faith in Christ and fall away from the Christian faith.

5. Get specific by looking at both family bloodlines and noting the afflictions that have befallen the members. Prayerfully address all physical infirmities and behavior issues.

6. Heed your child's requests for prayer. Directly pray over those areas. If you need to ask for forgiveness from your child for some past grievance, this is a good time to do it.

7. Together, ask the Lord for guidance and direction in your time of prayer to be certain you haven't missed anything.

8. The finale: Affirm your child and tell them you are proud of his or her accomplishments thus far in life. Instill confidence that God has something wonderful planned for their lives. Emphasize that it takes truth and courage to do His will, and that their walk with the Lord will be an adventure. Give your young adult a small memento of this special day such as an inscribed Bible or a book.

THE CURSES ON BROOKE HAVE BEEN BROKEN

Brooke was very appreciative of our get-together. She valued our time and intention. We prayed, talked, cried, and shared for hours. Brynne had a very similar experience three years earlier. Both girls took very seriously what this day meant. During this precious time it seemed as though, in a way, they grew up before our eyes when they realized what it means to stand in your own faith as an adult. I hope they will always remember that day. I know that as a mother, I cherish these memories and, as of the writing of this book, we still have one more daughter to take through this highly valued time with the Lord.

On the birthday party day, I remember watching Brooke as she smiled and cut the cake with her friends. This significant birthday was not only bittersweet, but it also marked a very important day both legally and spiritually for Brooke. Thankfully, because our entire family understands the importance of waging spiritual warfare, she did not walk into this day blindly. Because of the knowledge she had gained by being raised in our home, Brooke knew the significance of breaking any curses over her life that would have been inherited and activated by her eighteenth birthday. While the balloons withered, the streamers were torn down, and the last of the stale cake was thrown out, supernatural reality would remain.

This is one more way to set your family free!

Chapter Nine

THE FAMILY PATH
TO PURITY

The first direct command ever given by God to humanity is summed in four simple words: "Be fruitful and multiply" (Genesis 1:28). This injunction to Adam and Eve comes right after their Creator, God, "blessed them." It's no stretch to conclude that God's initial instruction to the human family, consisting of just two at the time, was to engage in sexual intercourse. (That's the only way they could "be fruitful and multiply.") In other words, God said, "Have sex."

You heard me right. The first thing God told human beings to do was to have sex. It's understood that part of the purpose was to "fill the earth and subdue it." Procreation was the direct intent of this command. But inherent to the equation was the pleasure received by sexual conjugation. Lest any reader miss what Scripture is saying, the Lord God was telling Adam and Eve to make babies and enjoy the journey.

SHOULD SEX BE FUN?

For too long, the Church, whether through the glorification of celibacy or by spiritually exalting the contemplative life (nothing inherently wrong with either) relegated all the physically stimulating senses of sex to a dark place of lust and concupiscence. But it's clear from Scripture that the distinction of male and female was "blessed," and that the act of sexual intercourse was "blessed." That's why, in an effort to disqualify this blessing, Satan has no tried to marginalize sex to the confines of pleasure only, with no need of marriage.

Historic Christianity has played right into that plan by teaching a view of sex that has too often been prudish, legalistic, and unbiblical. Many Christians have reacted to the immorality of the world around them by separating sex from pleasure. They haven't done so explicitly, but the inherent message has been that the only way to be different from a fallen world is to avoid the attraction of sexuality, even in marriage.

This overreaction is somewhat understandable, because Christians in the early Church were surrounded by a Greco-Roman culture that promoted temple prostitution and ritual sex as a way of communion with the gods. The collateral damage was to ignore sexual pleasure as if it didn't exist. It did, but that didn't matter. "Better marry than burn" (1 Corinthians 7:9) was sloganized as a way of life for most Christians until the Reformation in 1517. It was none other than Martin Luther who brought back the idea that sex was for satisfaction as well as parenting. In his book *Luther's Fortress*, author James Reston, Jr. records that on one occasion Luther wrote to a doctor of canon law, "Kiss and rekiss your wife." He believed that celibacy would make one fall prey to "devouring fires and unclean ideas." Luther also pointed out that the Bible describes Isaac "showing endearment" to his wife Rebekah, a polite way of saying they were in the act.

The Bible does not say that sex and procreation must be separated; the Song of Solomon proves otherwise. Amidst its explicit sexual descriptiveness (e.g., "your two breasts are like two fawns," 4:5) there is no mention of children. There is no suggestion that all the intense love-making was to produce offspring only, and that any pleasure derived was merely a by-product of keeping the "fruitful and multiply" command.

Unleashing Sexuality from Unbiblical Ideas

What does this mean where setting the family free is concerned?

Modern Christians must decide whose side they are on. Our counseling experience tells me that many, if not the majority, of married Christian couples have unwittingly adopted a fourth-century view of sexuality. (Church father Jerome declared in the fourth century, "Anyone who is too passionate a lover with his own wife is himself an adulterer." And the catechism of the Catholic Church in 1494 declared that enjoying sex within marriage was a deadly sin.) Will evangelical couples now side with Protestant reformers who rejected the ideal of ascetic sexuality, as do enlightened Catholic theologians today? Or will they carry on as if it didn't matter when the flame of love burns low? When sexual frequency wanes and even ceases, does either spouse flash a warning signal that something is desperately wrong in the marriage? Why don't Christian couples see this as the harbinger of potential sexual and emotional affairs?

We must free the family from both antiquated and unbiblical thinking about romantic love and sexual pleasure, which includes considerably more than just the act of intercourse, and from the modern fundamentalist ascetics who never met a romantic activity that they didn't dislike, from dating to mere hand-holding.

In our opinion, the greatest threat to Christians embracing the idea of sexual pleasure doesn't come from cultic abstinence or old-school Catholicism. It's found in the new crowd of evangelical puritans who eschew all forms of touch or romance prior to marriage. As parents of three daughters who interact with conservative Christians, we have seen firsthand the effect these new holier-than-thou teachings have had on young lives. We believe that we must free the family to include authentic sexuality as part of the marriage relationship, and that we should extol healthy sexual discussions as part of the child-rearing process.

In His Sermon on the Mount, Christ declared, "Blessed are the pure in heart, for they shall see God" (Matthew 5:8). Like most, I generally thought of this passage as referring to living a godly life and then seeing God in eternity as the result. But the Holy Spirit has enlightened me to understand that this Bible verse means more. For a moment, take the emphasis off the "pure in heart" and give attention to "they shall see God." This is not limited to an eternal perspective. The pure in heart will also see Him in the here and now. With spiritual eyes they will see the path to successful living which is not hindered by the damage of sexual sin. They will see God and avoid the suffering of sexually transmitted diseases. They will see God and know to eschew tangled relationships that are controlling and abusive. They will see God and thus have the ability to wisely choose a lifetime mate with whom to walk in obedience to Christ. And they can only accomplish these goals if they are pure in their hearts.

With this goal of moral righteousness in mind, what follows is practical advice on keeping children in the family pure in their moral lives. Because we have three daughters, I defer now to Laura to discuss some healthy ways that a purity process can be introduced to children in a wholesome way.

How to Lead Children on the Path to Sexual Purity

Three of the most memorable times I ever shared with my daughters in more than twenty-two years of parenting were three special weekends planned for each of the girls individually. These "purity weekends" happened soon after puberty. We set aside time to go away on a trip to a place of their choice. We didn't go to enjoy an exciting destination. Our purpose was to delve into an important aspect of their lives—understanding and maintaining their pure, sexual identity. It was a time to focus directly on each of the three as individuals who were coming into adulthood. We discussed all matters that are crucial to physical, emotional, and spiritual development. During this Mom-and-daughter time we talked about God's perfect plan for their sexuality and the boundaries that He has established to protect them, value them, and prepare them for a healthy marriage.

All the girls now agree that, even though the weekends were intense and a little uncomfortable at times, their purity weekend was a notable occasion and they felt special. We talked, laughed, and, most important, we seriously discussed God's plan for them as women. We discussed how they would have to determine their own way forward on this path. We considered soberly what would be required to navigate this challenging time of adolescence and moving toward womanhood. In particular, I wanted to make sure that they fully understood God had a plan for their lives, His wisdom is supreme, and they would choose the Bible as their road map for living.

With the goal in mind, I began by refreshing things that I had previously taught them about how to establish true wisdom and understanding. Long before the weekends, we had talked about how God has given us commandments, not to punish us, but for our own good and moral self-preservation. When we look at His moral laws and the wisdom of His Word, we can see how these truths help us navigate through a sinful world. I countered the destructive narrative that God is cruel and that we can't trust Him. I emphasized that the message of the Bible will never change and never let us down. I explained that people who violate the Bible eventually sear and destroy their own souls and that much later in life these people are often forced to admit their mistakes, many realizing too late how much they should have appreciated God's direction and should have listened to the Christian teachings of their parents.

Planning and executing the purity weekend. Before the purity weekend, I prayed that each girl's heart would be in the right place to properly receive what I would tell them. I purchased an excellent set of resources entitled *Passport2Purity* by Dennis and Barbara Rainey of Family Life Ministry (available in most Christian bookstores or online at http://www.familylife.com/passport2purity). I appreciate the program that the Raineys have developed. It's a comprehensive plan that walks a parent and child through a purity weekend. They even consider ways to allow time for a fun activity break; in our case, one daughter chose skiing, one horseback riding, and another shopping.

In the *Passport2Purity* program, there is a preparation section that tells you everything you need to purchase and bring on your trip, and it even provides a time schedule. It includes CDs that you and your child listen to, which are very entertaining and dramatized specifically for this age group. (The age they recommend is preadolescence, but we chose to have our weekends a little later.)

Here's a quick overview of the weekend: You and your child follow the schedule, listen to the CDs, and do the activities that they have prepared. It is nice because you are listening together. Then you discuss what your child has understood. That fun activity is to be scheduled right after the CD that explains (on their age level) the meaning and methods of having a marital sexual relationship, and that timing is perfect, because the child feels a little uncomfortable and needs a break.

More than sex is addressed. The morality and sexual choices available in our world are explained. In *Passport2Purity,* the Raineys deal with the physical and biological aspects of sexual reproduction. They also cover controversial subjects such as masturbation and its relationship to moral purity. They explain how to develop personal convictions when deciding what to do and what not to do. There are no apologies for the belief that the Bible is to be the child's guide and source of wisdom; that bad friends can create a herd mentality that is tough to resist; that it is important to guard healthy innocence, to keep passion and natural desire under control by not igniting it until marriage; that purity is not renewable; and that each person they have a sexual relationship with leaves a mark on their lives.

We discussed things frankly so that they would not be blindsided but would know what to expect. There were some rather squeamish areas, and I did my best to answer some tough questions. I appreciated the way the program gave the girls a proactive approach to their lives and choices. Some parents might say, "Oh, kids probably know more than we do because of the Internet." But that does not give us as parents an excuse not to teach our children the correct approach to sexuality based on what the Bible says. In fact, their notions of sexuality might be totally skewed because of what they have inadvertently seen online.

The heart-warming weekend comes to a close. I have no hesitation saying that those purity weekends with my daughters were so worth it. I invested time and money and focused an entire weekend on each daughter, which made each one feel special and valued. At the end of the weekend, each girl was given her own facsimile of a passport to sign, signifying her decision to follow up on what she had learned.

We also invited Bob to join us at a closing meal to talk about what had gone on for the two-plus days. Each time, Bob showed up looking spiffy in a sport coat and slacks. We dined at a special candlelit restaurant. Bob wrote each of the girls a letter about how dearly he loved them and what they, and this weekend, meant to him. He said that he wished that his parents would have had a weekend like this for him when he was a young boy. He thought it was such a tremendous idea and was almost as excited as I was, even though he was only invited to attend at the end.

As we dined, there was a unique, emotional closeness that we all felt. Having each daughter conclude the time with their father was a special treat. They shared the decisions that they had made, and Bob laughed about some of the funny stories that had happened during the weekend. At the very end of the night we presented each girl with a beautiful purity ring she had chosen in advance. This ring symbolized her choice to walk with Christ in sexual purity. It also signified their understanding of how much they are loved by God and us. I am only sad that I don't have any more children with whom to experience one of these weekends.

My youngest daughter and I completed her purity weekend this year. Family Life Ministry has a similar program for fathers and sons. The Lord chose not to give us a son, so Bob didn't get to experience the pleasure of sharing a similar experience firsthand. Mothers and fathers of younger children still have these special memories to look forward to.

Adding spiritual warfare to the purity paradigm. In addition to the excellent program offered by Family Life, I had some additional spiritual warfare aspects to share with our daughters. Much about this topic is simply understanding the basic truths of God's Word, but it is also important to have specific information to be wise about the enemy's tactics. One area ripe for attack from Satan is the arena of how our children are educated.

We chose to homeschool all three of our children, not so much because we wanted to shield them from the harsh realities of life in our fallen world as because of three wonderful, persistent ladies who kept encouraging me to homeschool. These women shared their love of homeschooling with me and encouraged me to seriously consider it for our family. I remember thinking, "That is great for you, but I can't do that." Finally, I "got it."

Little did I know when I started my homeschooling journey seventeen years ago that I would make it to the finish line, and I would have never guessed that our personal homeschooling curriculum would include traveling around the world for social studies, accompanying Bob on various missions overseas. The best part of this special benefit was that the girls served others alongside their family. If they had been in school, they would have missed that opportunity.

I could not and did not shield them from the realities of life in ministry. I felt that I should be realistic with my children to prepare them for life. Consequently, they heard all kinds of stories from people in nation after nation who sought ministry for relief from Satan's attacks. After watching Bob and me minister deliverance and exorcism in dozens of countries, seeing demonic forces intent on their destructive mission openly manifesting and being confronted by the power of

Christ, and after hearing stories and witnessing victories over evil, they were fully convinced that the devil is real and is to be avoided in every way possible.

Bob has always encouraged people to deal with the truth, if they want to be free from Satan. He emphasizes many times the words of Christ: "And you shall know the truth, and the truth shall make you free" (John 8:32). The truths that our children have heard might have shaken some families, but not our children. We had prepared them to understand how active the devil is in attempting to ruin peoples' lives. Our children have been on the front row night after night, hearing how women ran away from home and became prostitutes and how people had sex outside of marriage and were devastated by it. Some of these individuals were filled with rage and murderous thoughts; others had tried to take their own lives; many had been sexually abused as children; others had lives filled with addiction.

The message to our children was clear. When people step outside of God's plan for purity, people are hurt. The girls saw firsthand the result of disregarding God. Life without the Lord isn't a party. It isn't fun or sexy. It is heart-wrenching. They saw so many Christian kids who danced on the boundaries of sin, somehow thinking they weren't cool unless they were rebellious and had a bad attitude. They learned that this is the cry of the herd mentality and that it comes from toxic people.

I am thankful that the Lord led us to be honest with our children with great care and understanding and teach about how He protects us and watches over us if we allow Him. How much happier children they will be and what greater chances for success in marriage and life they will have, because they have been persuaded to heed the words of God: "Therefore you shall love the Lord your God, and keep His charge, His statutes, His judgments, and His commandments always" (Deuteronomy 11:1).

Chapter Ten

THE FACTS ON THE
FACTS OF LIFE

(Warning: Chapter includes sexually explicit material)

Among the main reasons for divorce, sexual incompatibility is always listed in the top five. Often it is the number one reason that couples split, even though it may not be the reason they give overtly. In our many years of intervention in troubled marriages, we've discovered that it is often the one topic that no one wants to discuss. Therefore, in the interest of addressing this understated issue, we decided to include this straightforward section in *Set Your Family Free*. To set families free we must liberate Christian couples from false assumptions about sexuality and sexual activity.

After helping many couples with sexual dysfunction, we've discovered that there are seven common challenges concerning intimacy that must be faced, especially in the Christian home:

1. Differences in expectations of intimacy regarding frequency of sex and techniques of intercourse and foreplay.

2. Unresolved emotional issues from bad sexual experiences prior to marriage, or sexual trauma experienced in a previous marriage.

3. Stress from financial strains, vocational demands, or family problems.

4. Unfaithfulness of one or both partners.

5. Unhealthy perceptions about sex resulting from how individuals were raised, particularly negative religious notions.

6. Inadequate or inaccurate information about all aspects of sexual activity.

7. Religious mores that may have marginalized sex or relegated it to procreation alone.

Each of these misconceptions and misunderstandings must be frankly addressed. To do so comprehensively isn't possible in a book of this length. Other Christian books have adequately discussed various ramifications of these seven challenges. Some books which the reader may find helpful are *Sex for Christians: The Limits and Liberties of Sexual Living,* by Lewis B. Smedes; *For Fidelity: How Intimacy and Commitment Enrich our Lives,* by Catherine M. Wallace; *Good Christian Sex: Why Chastity Isn't the Only Option—And Other Things the Bible Says About Sex,* by Bromleigh McCleneghan; *Intended for Pleasure: Sex Technique and Sexual Fulfillment in Christian Marriage,* by Ed Wheat; *The Act of Marriage: The Beauty of Sexual Love,* by Tim and Beverly LaHaye. The Focus on the Family ministry also has excellent materials on all aspects of human sexuality as it relates to Christian faith. We do not necessarily endorse every conclusion and viewpoint of these authors and books. Readers must determine individually whether the advice offered is helpful and biblical.

We will focus on the five areas of sexuality that, from our experience, are most troubling to Christian couples. We do not suggest that what follows is the complete or final word on these topics, but we pray it will be a starting point of discussion for couples in sexual crisis.

CATEGORIES OF SEXUAL CONDUCT NEEDING CLARIFICATION

Pornography. With the easy accessibility of pornography, it is all too common for Christian couples to experiment with porn in an attempt to spice up a dull, married sex life. I have encountered even pastors who insisted on making their wives watch XXX-rated videos with them, with the intent of having the wife duplicate the actions seen on-screen. How demeaning is that? Even in the privacy of the bedroom can such actions be considered acceptable? Never. It's a form of adultery or virtual ménage à trois, with another sexual partner in the marriage bed. If either or both of the marriage partners use pornography as an aide to improve sex, this situation telegraphs a sad state of disrepair in the realm of sexual communication. Keep far away from anything that can lead to pornography. Do not attempt to explore demonically induced fantasies, which can propel an individual from the real world of real sex into a make-believe realm that leads to increasing forms of deviant stimulation. Good resources are available to combat influences from the hypersexualization of our society.[6] Pornography is an ever-escalating path to sexual desensitization, the eventual numbing of all normal sexual desire—and addiction to its stimulation. It's sexual slavery. Don't get caught in it!

A further warning: When your spouse finds out that you have been indulging in pornography behind her or his back, your marriage is on the way to disintegration. And, yes, from my experience as a deliverance minister there is a demon who assumes the nominal designation, Spirit of Pornography. He may claim the legal right of entry and possession of the individual who views even the smallest amount of porn, especially where there is a generational curse of lust.

One more thought: Shame and guilt are usually not enough to rescue a porn addict. Most Christians I've counseled tell me that they've tried that route of remorse, then repentance, then relapse, then remorse again, then repentance again, then relapse again, and so on, many, many times. It usually doesn't work. What's often needed is intervention by an addiction specialist. When the bondage to erotic images is demonic (and it often is), deliverance prayers are needed to remove the tormenting spirits that feed on this obsessive predilection.

Impotency. In clinical terms, erectile dysfunction (ED) is the inability of a male to maintain an erection of the penis both before and during sexual intercourse. Physiologically, an erection is attained and maintained by blood entering tissue in the penis. The process results from messages sent by the brain upon sexual arousal. When an erection does not occur or cannot be maintained sufficiently for sustained intercourse, the cause may be medical or psychological/relational. Common physically systemic causes include heart disease, diabetes, hormonal imbalances, alcohol or drug inhibitors, or neurological problems. Psychological factors may be connected to one's past sexual history, upbringing, or previous emotional trauma related to sexuality, such as molestation experiences.

A medical doctor should be consulted, particularly a urologist, to determine what physical factors may be contributing to the condition. If that avenue of help isn't successful and the problem is not strictly related to body malfunction, other professional help is necessary. Relational issues may develop if a marriage is troubled and emotional connection is inhibited. Most clergy are not adequately informed and trained to handle such matters; consequently, a licensed professional should be sought. I have spent many years helping couples with such matters and have educated myself in this area, but most individuals in ministry would not possess a sufficient knowledge base. However, if help is sought outside the church, care must be exercised when choosing a sex therapist, since their advice may have no biblical basis and may include sinful suggestions such as pornography, erotic massage, or the intervention of a sexual surrogate (a nice way of saying therapeutic prostitution).

Common spiritual reasons for ED that I encounter with ministry clients are: (1) excessive, obsessive masturbation that may gradually shut down responses to normal sexual intercourse, (2) pornography, which over time raises the threshold of sexual arousal to a level that can't be sustained during ordinary sexual stimulation, (3) previous lustful fantasies that intrude on the mind during marital sex, (4) past sexual abuse which wired the brain to respond to sex only in a vulgar context, and (5) a highly promiscuous lifestyle before Christian conversion, which deprived the body of its ability to function without the thrill of conquest and quickly performed coitus.

As a deliverance minister, I do find that some ED is related to demonic interference on a sexual level, requiring expulsion of the evil spirit. Yet I caution that such a spiritual conclusion should not be reached without first eliminating other factors, as already explained. Demons typically associated with sexual dysfunction, including ED, may be Jezebel, Abuse, Molestation, Lust, Incest, and Rejection.

Masturbation. There is no clear biblical prohibition against masturbation (autoeroticism), which is the practice of sexually stimulating one's one genitals, usually to the point of orgasm. The most common objection of Christians is that autoeroticism is generally associated with pornography and erotic fantasies; however, this is not always the case. In the absence of a biblical prohibition, some turn to the story of Onan in Genesis chapter 38 when God judged Onan for having "spilled his semen on the ground." But a clear reading of this passage shows that Onan's sin was not masturbation, but rather disobeying the Lord's command to produce offspring on behalf of his brother's widowed wife by interrupting intercourse. Interrupted intercourse, especially when used as a form of birth control, though not necessarily advisable, does not usually constitute masturbation.

Outside of marriage, the lust and mental imagery necessary to achieve arousal to masturbate is inappropriate. Within marriage, masturbation as a substitute for coitus may be considered sexually defrauding, if it is used as a means of convenience in place of intimate communication.

Sometimes, the ability to consummate vaginal intercourse is compromised by the prolonged, habitual practice of masturbation on the part of the male. This is medically and psychologically known as "retarded ejaculation." Other dangers are skin irritation from so-called "rough masturbation" and even penile fracture due to rupture of the chambers that fill with blood during an erection.

There may be times in a marriage when, due to health reasons, masturbation by mutual consent is acceptable, such as when physical impairment prevents coitus. It may also be used as a means of foreplay to achieve sexual arousal, if it does not lead to full sexual release. But such actions shouldn't be considered the normalized form of sexual performance due to the negative spiritual and physical consequences. Some years past, a controversial Christian writer opined, "When single people get to heaven, they will thank the Lord for the gift of masturbation as a means of keeping sexually pure." I mince no words to label that idea as misguided, ill-informed, and spiritually dangerous.

I have been asked, "Is there a demon of masturbation?" Yes, I've encountered many evil spirits that claim that designation. That doesn't mean all masturbation is demonic and that autoerotic arousal will lead to demonization. It may, but the demonization is usually due to the accompanying pornography or other lustful add-ons. Though getting a demon by masturbation is certainly a possibility that I have documented in many cases, the biggest concern should be the loss of self-control to what can easily become an addiction. It's a bad habit not easily broken, even by sex in marriage. If the reader is contemplating marriage, whether you are male or female, conquer this consumptive habit now before it ruins your marriage bed later.

Oral sex and sexually transmitted diseases. Clinically stated, oral sex is any sexual activity that involved the stimulation of the genitals of one's partner using the mouth and/or tongue. Cunnilingus refers to oral sex performed on females while fellatio refers to oral sex performed on males. It is used by some couples as part of foreplay before sexual intercourse, or it is practiced as a form of intercourse during which either the male or female, or both, achieve orgasm. As with masturbation, there is no clear biblical prohibition, no "thus saith the Lord."

We must, therefore, look at other guiding principles for the Christian marriage bed. An important factor to consider is to what extent one's spouse is comfortable with any particular sexual technique. Good sex, biblical sex, is about mutual emotional safety. A husband or wife should not insist on their spouse engaging in any sexual approach which the other considers distasteful or disagreeable, even if the aversion to certain sexual methods may be the result of bad information or spiritually unsupportable notions of moral virtue.

Some questions to consider are these: Is the sexual activity being forced upon an unwilling mate? If so, that isn't a loving act. Is one partner violating a personal comfort boundary of the other? That isn't right.

A distinction should be made between oral sex as a means of foreplay and arousal as opposed to oral sex leading to consummation. The former may sometimes be acceptable, based on the principles established above. But as a means of sexual consummation on a regular basis, it fails to fulfill the proper sexual needs for which God intended vaginal penetration. Oral orgasm, as a dominating part of a couple's sexual behavior, to some extent alters the one-flesh intimacy for which God has designed the male and female body. It certainly alters the "knowing" (Genesis 4:1) principle of sex, wherein eye and facial contact take place during lovemaking. There may be irregular instances in which oral sex leading to orgasm between married couples is permissible if one or both partners is permanently disabled, for example, with quadriplegia, from engaging in vaginal penetration.

Some in deliverance ministries speak of a demon of oral sex. Such an evil spirit would not necessarily be acquired by foreplay stimulation. It is more likely connected to a perverted view of sex, which is exploitive and narcissistic.

Another important consideration is knowing whether one's sexual partner, even in marriage, is HIV-positive or has a genital sexual disease.

Even in a Christian marriage, one or both of the partners may have been sexually active before marriage without using protective measures. Knowledge of any sexually transmitted diseases should be disclosed prior to marriage. I understand the fear of this being a deal-breaker, but that possibility must be faced truthfully and not hidden. I've counseled Christian couples where one of the partners contracted an STD from marital sex because their spouse came into the marriage with the disease. When it wasn't disclosed beforehand, deep anger and bitterness is often the result. Better to be honest and call off the marriage than to suffer through a divorce based on sexual misrepresentation.

Of perhaps greater concern is the possibility of getting throat cancer, which, according to a study published in *The New England Journal of Medicine,* is likely to happen if there has been ejaculated, oral sex with at least six different people.

Sadomasochism and anal sex. Aberrant forms of sexual activity involving anal penetration and the inflicting of pain or humiliation to received sexual pleasure should be considered off limits by Christians, even when there is mutual consent. Such forms of sexual activity represent a disordering of the principles of sexuality set forth in Scripture. Sex in the Bible, as we've already pointed out, is based on a love principle of treating one's spouse as they would their own body. As the apostle Paul pointed out in Ephesians 5:28, no one ever hated his own body, unless that individual was deranged. Would a person deliberately seek to inflict pain, control, domination, and shame over his own body, unless he was mentally ill? The rhetorical answer is, "No!" Then why would it be acceptable to do it to another person? Ephesians 5:25 states emphatically that a husband should be willing to die for his wife, as Christ died for the church. That is a high standard of how to treat one's spouse that cannot include the inflicting of suffering or humiliation.

"What of playful pain?" some have asked. I've had Christian couples insist that the acting out of dominance, submission, and humiliation makes sex more interesting. What of a Christian woman assuming a dominatrix costume or role? If it's between consenting adults, they say, what's the problem?

We would point back to the focus of sex as set forth in the Scripture. It is to give pleasure to one's love-mate in Christ, not to seek thrills for one's personal gratification. Most sadomasochistic tendencies form in early childhood out of child sexual abuse such as incest and molestation. How tragic that some in the psychological community, which once considered S&M to be a sociopathic personality disorder, now view it as acceptable, so long as it is not excessively violent.

The same is true for anal sex; barriers against this deviant sexual technique have also fallen, even among some Christians. When couples ask me if it's acceptable, I merely reply, "Look at the plumbing, notwithstanding the sanitary concerns, and ask yourself why anyone would subvert the obvious intent of the human anatomy for the sake of exploratory curiosity?"

Final Thoughts about Christian Sexuality

There are no "fifty shades of grey" when it comes to biblical sex. No ambiguous areas allowing for stimulation by means of abnormal erotomania without boundaries of mutual respect and loving consideration. Sex in marriage begins in the heart, not the genitals or with stimulating sex toys. God wants to heighten sexual pleasure in marriage, not diminish it by things that lead to jadedness and dissatisfaction.

It is clear from Scripture that the Lord has condemned rampant, uncontrolled sexual desire outside of marriage (see 1 Corinthians 6:18). God wants sex in marriage to be good, not crude. God destined sex to populate the earth and bring pleasure to His people, not be the subject of raunchy comedies or the source of four-letter words.

It's impossible to give a complete list of all the impermissible forms of sexual temptation. No sooner would the list be finished, when Satan and technology would have created yet another open door for spiritual bondage. Cohabitation with lifelike robots? Sex via virtual reality? In a world in which the U.S. commercial sex industry has larger revenue than the National Football League, National Basketball Association, and Major League Baseball combined, money is no object to overcoming any technological barrier to a more stimulating and financially lucrative sex market. I'm certain that Satan has a sexual agenda beyond any which the brightest Silicon Valley entrepreneur could dream about.

For Christians to navigate around this moral cesspool that tries to seep into Bible-based homes, we must keep sound scriptural admonitions in mind. Consider these:

> *All things are lawful for me...but I will not be brought under the power of any.* (1 Corinthians 6:12)

> *All things are lawful for me, but not all things are helpful; all things are lawful for me, but not all things edify.* (1 Corinthians 10:23)

> *Abstain from every form of evil.* (1 Thessalonians 5:22)

> *Do not give the devil a foothold.* (Ephesians 4:27, NIV)

The heart is the door to temptation and every evil invasion. If you are married, flirting with that man/woman at the office, fantasizing on Facebook, or checking out arousing images on your cell phone may be all that Satan needs to gain entry to your soul. Follow biblical principles and the other precepts set forth in this book and your family will be set free, by the power of Christ!

ENDNOTE

1. Our ministry has produced a three-hour teaching series on pornography, available on DVD, which can be purchased from our web store at www.boblarson.org.

Chapter Eleven

ANSWERS FROM THE HEART OF A MOTHER

Those who seek our help are often sincere people who haven't received adequate teaching regarding how to handle the more difficult questions of family life. Even though many wonderful Christian books have been written and helpful seminars conducted by ministries dedicated to assisting families, these individuals who reach out to us haven't been aware of the wealth of resources available. More important, whatever help or advice they have gotten didn't include a perspective that understands the deviousness of the devil and the need of deliverance prayer. Here are some of the more common questions about troubled family life that come our way.

Must there always be agreement with all family members regarding standards and practices? How can a family live in harmony and spiritual agreement? Healthy family dynamics allow for differences of opinion between spouses, and also between parents and children. Foundational biblical truth isn't open to dispute for the Christian family. For example, everyone in the family would agree with the scriptural teaching that

Jesus is the Son of God and the Savior of the world. From time to time our family has studied the historic creeds such as the Nicene Creed and the Apostles' Creed. Beyond such bedrock standards, family members might disagree on things such as:

- Bedtime on holidays,
- Which church best suits all family members,
- When mealtimes will be scheduled,
- Which meals are "family time" and not excusable,
- When and where to take family vacations.

Make a list of what agreements are negotiable and which ones are not. Sometimes it is impossible to have all members agree, for example, upon where to go for dinner; but if all family members agree with the family mission statement (see below), then everything can line up under those principles. Changes can be made, but consistent standards and practices will be a strong foundation for a home.

A family mission statement is a declaration in a paragraph or so that summarizes a family's beliefs and goals. Such a statement might include:

- What are nonnegotiables for our family?
- What is the most important goal for our family?
- What core beliefs do we stand for?
- What binds us together in unity?
- What will we not allow to harm our family?

I am thankful that our family has adhered to our mission statement. That's not to say it has always gone unchallenged. We have had many heated discussions and debates around our kitchen table. Thank the Lord it was the small stuff like cell phone usage. We have encouraged our children to have opinions and back them up. This can make it harder to reach decisions, but it is worth the time. Children need to learn how to make wise choices that are logical and have good reasoning behind them.

It is equally important to listen to children's opinions. Even younger family members can be encouraged to think through their requests. The more involved the family is in making decisions, the better their adherence will be. Do your homework before creating standards and make sure they are attainable. Someone has said, "Pick your battles when it comes to parenting."

A good question to ask your children when considering your family's mission is this: Will it make a difference ten years from now? If the answer is yes, it's time for a serious debate or a decision. If there is strong disagreement, who will make the family's final decision? Ultimately, a husband should be honored by the family, and his word carries weight. It is not good for the family to disregard the biblical principle that the husband is the head of the home. Furthermore, we need to pray for wisdom for our decisions and invite Christ to be the ultimate head of our homes.

What are some ways to encourage intellectual stimulation? Your children will copy what they experience at home. There are exceptions, but for the most part, you and your spouse's attitudes toward positive intellectual growth and social connectedness will have great influence on your children's attitudes. How can parents command a child to read a book if they themselves are binge-watching television? A well-intended encouragement for a child to read will come up blank when not modeled by the parents, and their behavior is often the greatest barometer for predicting what a child will choose.

Family intellectual discussions need to be engaging and to encourage thinking without having the parents act professorial. I enjoy it when my husband shares with our family something interesting that he has learned. He isn't intimidating, and he doesn't put anyone on the spot; but by his example, he encourages all of us to enjoy learning and acquiring knowledge. Our girls often ask Bob questions about his topic and engage in lively discussions; sometimes a discussion turns into an even livelier debate.

How can children be encouraged to engage in healthy socialization? Like parent, like child, typically. There are, however, temperamental differences that must be considered. Parents need to know on a basic level if family members are introverts or extroverts or somewhere in between. A quick definition of each: Introverts tend to recharge by spending time alone. They lose energy from being around people for long periods of time, particularly large crowds. Extroverts gain energy from other people. At the extreme ends of the spectrum, in other words, some people need downtime alone, while others thrive with constant socialization. This is a fundamental difference and can affect the ability to establish relationships. There may also be differences interpersonally as to how much time each child needs with other family members.

My husband and I differ in this category as he is more introverted that I am. Our children exhibit varying degrees of these introvert/extrovert temperaments. Sometimes you may wrongly expect your spouse to be the same as you are socially; but they may be wired differently. Don't be fooled into judging the degree of social engagement by one-on-one conversations. Bob seems very extroverted with me and loves nothing better than talking for hours on end. But he's not necessarily that way in small groups or social situations.

Despite these differences in personality type, all people need to develop and engage in a healthy social life. Christ set forth an important observation about friendship. Here are His words: "This is My commandment, that you love one another as I have loved you. Greater love has no one than this, than to lay down one's life for his friends" (John 15:12–13). Living that precept in action is a great challenge and an excellent way to evaluate the importance of socialization. Isolation is not a healthy state of being and is often spiritually dangerous.

Look for resources in Christian bookstores and online sites. One resource that is valuable in understanding the personalities of your spouse and children comes from the Myers & Briggs Foundation.[7] Their system, based on solid psychological research, is used widely in business by human resource departments. It is somewhat complicated, but also fascinating.

How are interactive family codes of conduct established? The best answer for this question is to involve the entire family in creating these codes. Try this. Arrange for the family a favorite dinner with everyone present. Establish a calm atmosphere, and have a list of questions prepared for the members about what family codes they think are important. Listen and document their answers and requests.

After dinner, begin with prayer, and then ask the questions you've compiled. You will probably find out quickly what is important to your children. Flexibility with strong moral standards is a good place to start. Remember to uphold nonnegotiables as we've already discussed. And don't start this process unless you can follow through with it. Begin by establishing that your family will honor God in everything and conduct themselves in a way that reflects the fruit of the Spirit.

Here are some guidelines for your discussions about codes of family interaction:

- Wait until one person is finished talking before speaking. Be polite and respectful of others.
- Talk about what is important to you without blaming others. Use "I" statements and not accusatory "you" references.
- No Internet usage after a certain hour.
- Parents have access to personal phone records, such as text messages.
- Honor one another and your parents with actions and words.
- No obscene or profane curse words allowed.
- Establish expectations for how family members act in public.
- Respect the private time of other family members.

- Define housework expectations, such as rotating schedules for chores.

- Know in advance what visitors and friends will be welcome in the home.

How does a defined code of conduct support what is important to families? Here are some goals that you should aim for: seeking God's will for the family, developing ways to love family members and learn from each other, providing a safe place to develop skills necessary for succeeding in life, being kind to others and thoughtful in every action, knowing how to pray for each other and remain submitted to Christ, creating a healthy emotional environment for all family members to grow without judgments or harshness.

How does a Christian family maintain proper principles without being repressive or legalistic? Families need to avoid any type of legalism. It is the number one reason that children later rebel and sometimes falter in their faith. Legalism can be defined as strict adherence to law, especially to the "letter of the law" rather than the spirit behind it. Legalistic theology teaches that salvation is gained through good works and adherence to precise laws of behavior.

Jesus set us free from this type of mindset, as shown by his reaction to the Pharisees in Matthew (chapter 23). He scathingly rebuked them for their externalized criteria of spirituality: "Woe to you." He chided them for their behavior: "You...have neglected...justice and mercy and faith...you...appear beautiful outwardly, but inside [you] are full of dead men's bones....You also outwardly appear righteous to men, but inside you are full of hypocrisy and lawlessness." And that's just for starters. Read all of verses 23–36 to understand the full import of his condemnation of legalistic hypocrisy.

A dear pastor friend once told me that because of his many years of experience as a Christian leader he had come to believe that one of the worst plagues to infest the Body of Christ is legalism. He said it was tremendously damaging to the Christian spirit, causing some to fall along the way. Bob and I agree. We've known many people who grew up always being told that they could never do enough "good" in their religious environment. Legalism makes family members accuse each other judgmentally. Legalistic parents look for things that are wrong about a child instead of focusing on the child's good gifts that God has given them.

Bob has ministered to people for years who are the victims of legalism, and he has grieved with them over how it has damaged their lives. Some parents were genuinely well-intended toward their children, but the result was destructive because they wielded anachronistic, unreasonable rules.

People who get free from this bondage say that their parents didn't feel good about themselves; consequently, they communicated that outlook to their children as a form of control. People who are raised within a strict system maintained by a small community of people perpetuate limited lives and a stifling mentality—unless they break free.

Bob, who is an expert on cults and who has written one of the defining books on the subject, *Larson's Book of World Religions,* says that what some people have experienced, in the name of God, is a cult-like control that pits the inner group against the outside world. He calls it a "we versus they mentality." These people, unless freed from this way of thinking, pay twice; they are damaged by their upbringing and they in turn damage their own children.

Consider the example of a young man who has lived a wild life, indulging in drugs, sex, stealing. He may have been acting out in rebellion to his overly stern father. Then he gives his life to Christ and sheds the bondages of the old life. He is a new creation, but the years of hard living have taken a toll; he has missed a lot of healthy emotional, spiritual, and social growth. If he doesn't get the proper kind of ministry and counseling, he may behave emotionally like an addict, even without using the addictive substances. He tries to become stable, set down roots with a wife, and start a family.

Here is where the curse of legalism takes hold. When this young man tries to govern his own family, he only knows how to do it by insisting on adherence to strict rules, because rules have helped him maintain his sobriety. He fails to recognize that what was crucial to get him off drugs may not be a credible way to lead a family (despite his experience with his own father). He knows that it is critical for an addict to stay away from triggers that would cause him to start using again and that this requires strict rules for sobriety. Unfortunately, he translates this legalistic set of rules and punishments, designed to protect himself, upon his young children, who don't understand what's happening. They resent living under a legalistic system and end up rebelling. What started out as good thing for their father caused them to become rule-breakers; thus, the cycle of controlling behavior continues.

This sounds a bit dismal. But if people from a legalistic background can be educated in a larger context of social and spiritual interaction, there is freedom and restoration in Christ. This is yet another reason we have written this book; we desire to see families and individuals set free from this curse of legalism and the rebellion that it fosters.

What if parents aren't on the same page spiritually—whose choices prevail? One of the favorite books that Bob and I read together before we were married was *How to Get Engaged,* written by Bobb Biehl. (We referred to this book in an earlier chapter.) Biehl contends that, If there are major disagreements before marriage, they must be discovered before a commitment is made to share one's life with another. In addition, Bob and I believe that getting deliverance counseling before marriage will greatly reduce the likelihood of a crisis-level juncture in the marriage.

The most basic biblical principle regarding a marriage relationship is found in the apostle Paul's words:

> *For the husband is the head of the wife, as also Christ is the head of the church; and He is the Savior of the body.* (Ephesians 5:23)[8]

Husbands, love your wives, just as Christ loved the church and gave himself up for her. (Ephesians 5:25, NIV)

I may be a little traditional, but I believe in the power of these Scriptures. It is a blessing to know that my husband will take a godly stand in our home, but that he is also careful to take everyone into account when a family decision needs to be made. I knew he would be this kind of man when I married him. Sometimes the decisions he makes are tough and he is torn when there are serious questions not easily decided. He does not declare what we will eat for breakfast or what everyone must watch on TV. However, when making decisions such as where a child will attend college, we discuss the matter for days. Ultimately, I want him, as the head of the home, to give his thumbs-up to these types of choices. He really tries to take everyone into account and be fair. He has been known to stay awake at night over these decisions. This is why I love and trust him and why both of the Scriptures above are honored by our family.

What are constructive ways to manage a blended family? Like first-time couples, potential marriage partners with ex-spouses would benefit by reading a book such as *How to Get Engaged*. With children from one or both former marriages, the issues discussed previously in this section are more complex. After the potential spouses discover keys to preventing another broken relationship, the children should be included in an overview regarding what has been determined to be the most important issues. By addressing potential pitfalls early on, blended families may thwart what otherwise might be deal-breakers.

Have a future-family meeting including children from both sides and discuss issues that are relevant to their melding with step-siblings. Emphasize the godly foundation that the home will be built upon and the fact that every child's opinion matters. Be aware that teenagers sometimes have interesting timing where asserting their independence. Give the siblings from both families sufficient time to emotionally evaluate their new circumstances. And be patient.

Remember that a blended family may involve more than those who will live in the same household. Be prepared for that stepchild's weekend away with the former spouse. Also, if both child's parents remarry, there will be a patchwork of not only stepparents, but step-grandparents, plus a collection of extended family members that could include bloodlines from three or more directions. Jealousies, angry feelings, territorial battles, shifting loyalties, and stubborn alliances may result. Talk about demonic soul-tie potentiality! If ever a situation needed prayer, this is it.

Once again, a mission statement is helpful, crafted with as much agreement as possible. Get spiritual routines on the agenda early, and don't depart from them. Don't forget that successive marriages resulting from wounded relationships carry a lot of baggage, and a lot of curses. Spiritual warfare praying, curse-breaking, and deliverance are vitally necessary. So is intensive counseling and inner healing.

LAURA'S FINAL THOUGHTS

There isn't space enough in this book to deal with all the important questions that Bob and I face in our ministry to families seeking freedom. The list of questions we've faced is almost endless. But, here are a few additional questions that deserve at least brief attention.

What if a child is indulging in demonic things? If you haven't already established a spiritual warfare paradigm of family values, it's never too late to start. Make a list of off-limits activities and entertainment. Be specific. For example: No horror movies. No Ouija boards or divining devices of any kind. No yoga. No Harry Potter. All occult-themed movies are off-limits. If you've had lax standards, it will be easier to deal with a little stubbornness now than handle a demonically tormented child later. Above all, don't try this at home—deliverance, I mean. Read Bob's books, contact our ministry, or get in touch with some credible deliverance ministry.

What if domestic violence occurs? That answer is simple. Get the children and get out. No debates, no misplaced compassion, no discussions. Never put yourself at risk of a violent spouse, and never, never risk emotional or physical harm to a child. If you can't get a church representative or friend or family member to help you get out, then call the police or a domestic violence center. It is never OK to stay in living conditions which are threatening to health and safety. Don't let some well-meaning, but very misguided, pastor tell you to endure it for the sake of Christ or to save the marriage. There are other ways to seek marital remedy without being a captive punching bag.

What if sexual abuse such as incest occurs in the family? If it's a parent, then the same rules apply as for domestic violence. Don't stay under any circumstances. Whether it is the mother or father who is culpable, he or she has to go, or the other parent must take the children away. Authorities must be notified. Immediate crisis counseling must be sought. This is likely a demonic situation so treat it with that sense of seriousness.

What if a family member is spiritually dangerous? The choice of action will depend on how serious the situation is. Example: if your spouse is frequenting psychics or in a soul-connected relationship with a witch or occult healer of some kind, you can't let that pass. Take a strong stand and insist that the activity must terminate, or you'll have no choice but to separate until it's resolved. A spouse heavily involved in the occult is committing spiritual adultery, particularly if that spouse previously claimed to follow Christ. If the occult inclinations are less serious, such as reading horoscopes or watching occult-themed TV shows, the potential for danger is still there. Make sure that your children know you consider such activity wrong, without necessarily undermining your marriage partner in their eyes. Seek the advice of a godly pastor or counselor who can help you evaluate the seriousness of the situation. Bob and I have had to deal with many cases where a spouse is dabbling in demonic things and then passes on the spiritual oppression to the spouse and children. Don't act hastily, but don't fail to take some action. Our ministry, and other credible deliverance ministries, can help to give you guidance on the seriousness of what's going on and possible courses of action. Above all, pray for protection over yourself and your children.

ENDNOTES

1. www.myersbriggs.org
2. If you are a single parent then your word will be the final word, submitting to Christ as the head of your family.

Chapter Twelve

FAMILY PRAYERS TO SET YOUR FAMILY FREE

Among evangelical Christians, prayer may be the most talked-about but least acted-upon of any aspect of faith. One reason for this neglect is that many believers don't know how to pray or what to pray about. And if believing parents aren't comfortable praying, their children certainly won't be. Some parents are as uncomfortable talking to their children about prayer as they are discussing sex. That is an odd situation, especially when so much of Christian worship and church life is about prayer.

If families are to be free in every way, they must pray "without ceasing,"[9] that is, they must make prayer a natural and constant part of daily life. The prayers that we have set forth in this chapter are based on these presuppositions: (1) the biblical command to pray, and to pray with expectation, (2) the idea that prayer is both a remedial action, as in prayers of forgiveness, as well as an offensive strategy, as in spiritual warfare prayers.

Prayer may also be protective against crises such as illnesses or accidents. Prayer can bring comfort when one is faced with fear and attacks initiated directly by demonic forces. Curses can be renounced and broken as an expression of proactive prayers.

The prayers that follow are not intended to be all-inclusive. Also, please note that most of these prayers are stated in the plural but may be adapted to singular as needed.

These prayers provide examples for the reader to jump-start family prayer life. You may choose to pray these prayers as is, or you may put your own spin on a unique circumstance in your family. However you use them, do pray. Pray when things are going well, to thank the Lord for His protection and provision. Pray when it seems that all Hell has come against you, to resist the devil and make him flee (see James 4:7)! Eloquence is not as important as the condition of your heart as you cry out to the Lord with thanksgiving or for deliverance from a desperate trial.

PRAYER BY A HUSBAND FOR HIS WIFE

Heavenly Father, thank you for my wife, the life-partner who is your gift to me. Help us to walk in spiritual unity. Help me to fulfill the command of Ephesians chapter five, to love her as Christ loved the church, not sparing His own life. Teach me, Lord, how to give up myself for my wife, and to honor and cherish her as flesh of my flesh, bone of my bone. Show me how to value her more each day as a lover and a friend. Open my heart to hear what she says and know how she feels. Keep us strong as a couple during difficult times. Guide us in all our decisions regarding the upbringing of our children that they may grow to honor you in all things. Whatever curses or assignments of evil that Satan has directed against my wife, as her spiritual covering, I resist by the blood of Christ. Every curse of her ancestors I cancel because she now belongs to a new generational covenant beginning with our marriage. You have made me her head, and I speak on her behalf to cancel every evil assignment the devil intends to bring her harm. When any difficulty comes our way, help us to stand on your Word which declares that one may chase a thousand, but two can put ten thousand to flight (see Deuteronomy 32:30).

PRAYER BY A WIFE FOR HER HUSBAND

Heavenly Father, thank you for my husband who serves you as the head of our family, even as Christ is the head and Savior of the Church (see Ephesians 5:23). I pray that he would be directed by you and be attuned to your Word, for you, Lord, are the source of ultimate leadership in our home. Please provide him with your wisdom, knowledge, and discernment. Help me, Father, to accept your will as my husband leads us. May I reflect, with my actions, proper respect and healthy submission as you have revealed these principles in your Word (see Ephesians 5:22). Thank you that my husband is my dear friend and companion. Lead us to value our time together so that we may create unity within our family. I acknowledge that my husband is our family's protector and provider, and I pray blessings and favor over his endeavors and service. Thank you that you have created the companionship of husband and wife to grow a family together. May we always honor you and give you glory for the divine favor our family receives. Please bless my husband's labors and cancel all of Satan's plans against him and our family. Thank you for the blessings of our godly ancestors and cancel the curses of our ungodly forebears, by the power of your holy name. May there be no evil, generational propensities in our bloodline passed on to future generations. I ask that the protections of Psalm 91 abide with my husband as he serves you and our family each day. May our love for each other, and for you, Lord, grow stronger as we walk in your will.

Prayer by Parents for their Children

Heavenly Father, as husband and wife, we agree together on behalf of our children. You promised that if two or more agree, in Your Name, that you will hear and act upon our prayers (see Matthew 18:19). We first thank you for the wonderful gift of our children. We stand upon your word, recognizing that "children are a heritage from the Lord" (Psalm 127:3). Give us the grace to guide them wisely, discipline them prudently, teach them by example, and instill in their hearts a reverence for you and your Word. Together, as parents, we resist every plan of evil that Satan has devised against them. We cancel every assignment the devil directs toward them. In the place of these curses, we speak abundant blessing over their lives. Help us to guard our mouths when speaking to one another, and make us strong together to take authority over every design of the Evil One. If there are any curses in either of our bloodlines which might affect our children, we cancel them by the power of Christ and pass on to our children a new heritage of faith in Jesus as Savior and Lord.

Prayer Before a Child Becomes a Legal Adult

(May be spoken by agreement of both parents or individually by a single parent. The version below assumes a two-parent household but may be adapted by a single parent.)

Heavenly Father, our child, [insert name of child], will become a legal adult on [specify date of legal emancipation]. As his/her parents, we come to you, Lord, to speak on his/her behalf one final time before he/she reaches the age of majority. We understand from Scripture that his/her legal emancipation will also signify his/her spiritual release from our direct authority. Consequently, while we may yet speak on his/her behalf, we desire to release him/her from any spiritual bondage resulting from his/her inherited blood lines. We ask the Holy Spirit to trace back through our generations to the roots of any evil actions or curses which may affect the future of [insert name of child]. We declare any such curses and all these iniquities canceled, by the blood of Christ. We henceforth bequeath to [insert name of child] a destiny which is free from all spiritual disobedience of our ancestors. He/she is now free to make righteous choices in life without being hindered by any obstacles spiritually inherited. We now release him/her to your care, Lord, for the fulfilling of your purpose in his/her life. We ask the Holy Spirit to guide each of his/her decisions as an adult and for your presence to abide with him/her all the days of his/her/life.

PRAYER BY CHILDREN FOR THEIR PARENTS

Heavenly Father, help us be faithful to your Word which tells us to honor and obey our parents in the Lord (see Ephesians 6:1). Help us to resist the spirit of rebellion, which First Samuel 15:23 says is a form of witchcraft. Lead us to pray for our parents daily that they may be guided by you, Jesus, in each word of advice and every direction that they give to our lives. Give us a loving attitude when we don't understand the reasons for the rules and restrictions they place on our lives. Help us to give our parents the benefit of the doubt that their experience and life wisdom compel them to place boundaries on our actions, even when we don't agree with what they say. Let us not be led into temptations which will rob us of the purity and purposes for which you created us. And may we always be grateful for loving parents whose desire is to serve God and provide us with a godly example for our future.

PRAYER BY CHILD FOR SIBLINGS

Heavenly Father, thank you for my siblings. Thank you for choosing my siblings and placing them in my life in your sovereign will and plan. Please bless my siblings and honor our friendships, as we make plans for our futures. Help us to respect one another and be a blessing to each other. God grant me patience and understanding to love my siblings. Help me to honor you with my behavior toward my siblings. May we exhibit the fruit of the Spirit with our interactions. By your grace, I will be my brother's keeper, and I will stick closer than a friend. Make a special place in my heart for my siblings. Help us to pray, preserve and protect each other no matter what challenges we encounter. I resist every attack of the Enemy to hinder God's purposes and to cause any division, strife, or conflict in our relationships. I renounce the curse of Cain, who rejected your blessing of his brother. Help me to accept every favor you bestow on my siblings with Christlike love. Keep me from jealousy, envy, or unforgiveness toward any member of our family. May we all seek to follow your will in harmony with your Word.

Prayer by Family Together

Heavenly Father, as a family we gather before your throne. In your presence we declare our unity as parents and children, bound together as one in Christ to bring glory to the name of our Savior. As a family unit, we resist every temptation of the devil that would bring division into our midst. We stand steadfast against all dissension and confusion. Keep our family grounded in you and your Word. We pray one for another that, where one of us is weak, the others might be strong. Help us to avoid hard words and unkind judgments toward one another and to support each other in every trial and victory. Lord, place your holy angels around our home to protect and preserve our faith. And when any one of us stumbles, may the others lift the fallen one to be restored to family unity. We declare to the devil that we take seriously God's call to daily put on the full armor of God, as directed in Ephesians chapter six. Together, we are ready to wage war against all the powers of darkness to rescue souls who are lost without faith in Christ.

PRAYER BY PARENTS FOR ADOPTED CHILDREN

(May be spoken any time after the adoption has been legally ratified.)

Heavenly Father, by your grace, you have allowed us to be the adoptive parents of this child, your gift to us. We understand that what we've done, in a civil sense, mirrors what you have done for us spiritually, as described in Romans 8:15–23. Because of our personal faith in your atonement and resurrection, you have adopted us into the family of God and made us "heirs of God and joint-heirs with Christ." We acknowledge that your act of grace, to receive us as full members of your eternal family, is an emblem of what we now declare for the child we've adopted. We recognize that we are not the biological parents of this child; however, because the law has granted us full rights and responsibilities as if we had given birth to [insert name of child], we declare on his/her behalf the following spiritual affirmation: that he/she is free from the curses of his/her biological bloodlines as well as any inherited iniquities of our bloodlines. We proclaim for him/her all the blessing of a godly heritage in Christ. Because he/she was not accepted by his/her biological parents, we break any curses of abandonment or rejection which have fallen on him/her. We ratify all these things with the full civil and spiritual authority granted to us by the government of man and the kingdom of Christ.

PRAYER BY GRANDPARENTS FOR THEIR GRANDCHILDREN

Heavenly Father, we thank you for our wonderful grandchildren. Help us to love them in a way unique to our role as grandparents. May we encourage them and be a source of spiritual strength. We pray that they seek the kingdom of God early in life and make their personal relationship with you a priority. Because of our link in the ancestral bloodline, we break every curse passed on to our children and hence to our grandchildren. We realize that we do not have direct spiritual authority over our grandchildren; that responsibility lies with our children, until their offspring reach the age of majority. Nevertheless, we do exercise the power of prayer on behalf of our grandchildren so that the Holy Spirit will draw them toward Christian faith. By our prayers, we impede every intent of Satan; we also cancel any curses which were passed to our children, and grandchildren, before we were aware of the need to take such action. We release blessing on our grandchildren, as Proverbs 17:6 declares, "Children's children are a crown to the aged, and parents are the pride of their children" (NIV).

PRAYER BY A BLENDED FAMILY

Heavenly Father, thank you for bringing together our families to become one, by the commitment of marriage. Lord, what you have put together, let no man put asunder. We consecrate the lives of our children from previous marriages, that they may unite through mutual faith in Christ. Although our families of origin are not the same, our common bond is your Gospel and the pursuit of your will. We desire for you, Lord, to weave together the story of our future to bring blessing and favor to each of us. May we be one family, under heaven, growing together in unity. We break every curse from each family bloodline in Jesus' name. We ask you to close every open door to evil opened by all the ancestors from both family heritages. As we begin the process of sharing parents, please keep us from jealousy, the seeking of control, rebellion, all hurts from previous marital discord, territoriality of siblings, favoritism of parents, manipulation for dominance, and any other ungodly motives that would harm this divinely joined family. May we all unselfishly seek your destiny for the new bond of love we have found, and may we defer to one another in the spirit of humility and sacrifice.

ENDNOTE

1. 1 Thessalonians 5:17

ABOUT THE AUTHORS

BOB LARSON, a seasoned expert on cults, the occult, and super-natural phenomena and founder of the online International School of Exorcism, ministers across the world. He has ministered in more than one hundred countries and has appeared on most major TV networks. His ministry has been covered in print by *People, The Los Angeles Times, The New York Times, The Washington Post, The Financial Times,* and hundreds of other publications.

For twenty years, Bob hosted a nationally syndicated radio talk show, *Talkback with Bob Larson,* which was heard coast-to-coast across the United States and Canada. The two-hour program, broadcast live by satellite weekdays, featured tough topics others wouldn't touch. The weekly audience numbered in the millions. *The Real Exorcist,* a reality TV series in which he starred as a real-life exorcist, showcased Bob's spiritual quest to battle the devil around the world.

Bob Larson's YouTube Exorcism Channel has nearly ten million viewers. Hundreds of real-life exorcisms, captured on video in his seminars, are featured weekly. In addition, the channel also airs a popular feature known as *Ask the Exorcist.* Bob responds to questions e-mailed to him from scores of nations, including many Muslim and predominantly non-Christian countries.

Bob has established the Center for Spiritual Freedom in Phoenix, Arizona. This training center hosts periodic teaching sessions and special institutes. The Center also offers integrative emotional healing and spiritual deliverance for restoration to whole-person wellness. Some of the conditions addressed are: anxiety, emotional exhaustion, anger management, rejection and abandonment issues, spiritual oppression, and health challenges.

In his Spiritual Freedom Seminars, Bob draws upon his more than forty years of experience investigating the occult to reveal how evil influences people's lives. "The devil traffics in human suffering," Bob explains, "and we take people to the 'point of the pain' to discover where their souls have been scarred, allowing Satan to torment them. Exorcism is often part of the healing process."

Bob has developed one-on-one Personal Spiritual Encounter sessions conducted at the Center for Spiritual Freedom in Phoenix, Arizona, and weekend seminars in scores of cities worldwide. Each individual is extensively profiled spiritually, psychologically, and psychically to determine the source of their personal challenges. Bob also offers special full-day and half-day Intervention Intensive sessions for those needing urgent personal assistance. For the business community, he presents a specially adapted Spiritual Warfare Success Seminar, teaching the Four Stage of Success.

God has given Bob a vision to raise up Do What Jesus Did (DWJD) Spiritual Freedom Teams to fulfill the mission of Christ and "preach the Gospel, heal the brokenhearted, and set the captives free" (Luke 4:18). DWJD teams have been established in more than one hundred cities worldwide, and new teams are forming every week.

Bob has founded an international fellowship of scores of churches affiliated with the mission of Luke 4:18—the Spiritual Freedom Churches International (SFC). These congregations consist of Associated Churches (those churches already in existence) and Affiliated Churches (new congregations). Bob oversees these congregations, providing spiritual covering and direction. Offices of the Spiritual Freedom Church are in Denver, Colorado, and Edmonton, Canada.

The International School of Exorcism provides online education and certification for those interested in learning the spiritual calling of deliverance and exorcism. Thirty courses are taught via professionally produced videos and detailed study guides, all available 24/7 online. Course instruction includes church history of exorcism, biblical accounts of deliverance, an understanding of the psychological aspects of healing ministry, angelology, demonology, and mental illness versus demonization. Hundreds of students from dozens of nations have completed the intensive instruction.

Bob enjoys skiing, hiking, mountain biking, and golfing. He has climbed China's Great Wall, has walked to the top of Harbour Bridge in Sydney Australia, has parasailed from a five-thousand-foot cliff in New Zealand, and has scaled the twenty-thousand-foot-high summit of the world's tallest free-standing mountain, Africa's Mt. Kilimanjaro.

He has written thirty-six books, translated into more than a dozen languages. His handbook, *Larson's Book of Spiritual Warfare,* is an encyclopedic reference about demons, the devil, and deliverance, and represents a lifetime of research and experience.

Larson's Book of Cults is a standard reference encyclopedia at many colleges and seminaries, as is *Larson's Book of World Religions and Alternative Spirituality.* Other books include: *Demon Proofing Prayers, Curse Breaking, Jezebel, Dealing with Demons,* and *Set Your Family Free.*

Due to his many achievements, Bob Larson was recently awarded an honorary doctorate. He and his wife Laura have three daughters, Brynne, Brooke, and Brielle. The whole family shares Bob's passion to set the captives free. They reside in Scottsdale, Arizona.

LAURA LARSON has ministered alongside her husband, Bob Larson, for nearly twenty-five years. She has a great appreciation for the ministry of healing and deliverance, but her area of greatest interest has been inner healing. "It is miraculous to be a part of helping people to be set free and turn their lives around," she explains. "God can do amazing things in our hearts if we just invite Him to do the work."

Laura has traveled with her husband in ministry to places such as Australia, New Zealand, South Africa, Botswana, Latvia, Ukraine, Russia, France, England, Mexico, Korea, Japan, China, Germany, Canada, Italy, Antigua, and the Bahamas. "I should have taken my first bungee jump before I married Bob," she says with a smile. "It would have helped me to prepare for such an exciting leap of faith."

Daily life for Laura includes homeschool teaching duties, planning and supervising homeschool debate tournaments, and teaching creative writing. She has homeschooled all three of her daughters, two of whom are now in college. With one left at home, she stays busy with her educational responsibilities. Laura, who has a BS in journalism, worked for a time at the Colorado governor's press office. She also worked in the real estate industry. In her leisure time, she likes to ride horses and bikes, hike, ski, swim, play tennis, and read.

She expresses her admiration for what the ministry of her husband, Bob Larson, has accomplished in their years together. "Our mission provides us a challenging task—to walk with people as they face the darkest recesses of their lives. Through the power of Christ, they start breaking the bondage that holds them down. It's thrilling to see people truly helped and changed, not just temporarily. I love to see the families whose lives are put back together express their love and appreciation for one another. That brings profound joy."

For More Information
Spiritual Freedom Church International, Inc.
P.O. Box 36380
Denver, Colorado 80236
(303) 980–1511
bob@boblarson.org
www.boblarson.org